ORCHESTRATION

A Practical Handbook

McGRAW-HILL SERIES IN MUSIC
DOUGLAS MOORE, *Consulting Editor*

ATKISSON • Basic Counterpoint

CHASE • America's Music

RATNER • Music: The Listener's Art

WAGNER • Orchestration: A Practical Handbook

WAGNER • Band Scoring

Other titles in preparation

ORCHESTRATION

A Practical Handbook

BY JOSEPH WAGNER

McGraw-Hill Book Company, Inc.

NEW YORK   TORONTO   LONDON   1959

ORCHESTRATION: *A Practical Handbook*

Copyright © 1959 by the McGraw-Hill Book Company, Inc. Printed in the United States of America. All rights reserved. This book, or parts thereof, may not be reproduced in any form without permission of the publishers.

Library of Congress Catalog Card Number 57–8634

II

67655

To Dr. Howard Hanson
who helped
to make America conscious
of its music

PREFACE

The approach to the subject of orchestration in this handbook is at levels other than those found in existing treatises. The study plan has been designed to fit the range of experience and requirements of the average student of music. Specific comparative studies of compositional styles are given to establish corollary styles of orchestration. Special emphasis has been placed on the importance of establishing idiomatic orchestral textures and spacings, in particular to music originally for keyboard instruments, as a primary objective. Keyboard idioms and patterns are analyzed and classified in terms applicable to orchestral instruments. Most of the illustrative examples are carried through idiomatic scoring methods for each section of the orchestra, starting with the strings and culminating with full orchestra. The practical aspects of the subject as both a functional and a useful means of self-expression are also recognized.

A short survey of the evolutionary phases of orchestration serves to establish certain technical data. This material is indispensable for score reading and for an understanding of transpositions, the operating principles of wind instruments, and the irregularities of brass parts prior to the nineteenth century. Instruments are evaluated according to their independent and supplementary capacities, their playing characteristics and exceptional peculiarities and their interrelationships. The timbre, tonal strength, and weakness of each instrument is examined in the perspective of musical contexts covering a normal gamut of compositional styles and techniques.

Orchestration in any form is neither practical nor possible until and unless the purely technical elements of musical structure have been properly recognized, assimilated, and evaluated. This aspect of the subject as a prerequisite of scoring, per se, is recognized in this text as the very core of a sound, workable scoring technique. Exhaustive knowledge and understanding of orchestral instruments can be only of limited value without the correlation of this vital element. Extenuating factors of range, sonority, and texture become inseparably associated with mixed timbres and tonal weights once the musical structure has been idiomatically prepared for their arrangement.

Inasmuch as the applied study of orchestration requires accessible source material, music for piano or organ of all periods and styles serves this purpose, either as a substitute for, or as a supplement to, original compositional sketches. For the average student orchestrator, the use of keyboard music is of special significance since the general tendency is toward musical thinking in terms of the piano. In this connection, it is of more than passing interest to observe the unusual prolific activity of composers and orchestrators in transcribing keyboard music for orchestra. It is quite startling to realize that most of the orchestral works by Maurice Ravel were first written as music for the piano. Orchestral transcriptions of organ music, more especially of the works of Johann Sebastian Bach, likewise have become both numerous and accepted as a significant part of the orchestral repertory. In addition, interesting comparisons of settings of identical thematic materials are to be found in most concertos for piano and orchestra since the time of Mozart. These passages show clearly each composer's way of adapting his musical ideas to the differing idioms of the piano and the orchestra. In each instance, the composer's sketch or the orchestrator's use of keyboard music requires an approach with an understanding of the inherent differences in the resonance and structural factors of the source materials.

Because music for keyboard instruments, more specifically for piano, has certain well-established idioms and patterns, it is possible to isolate and classify these details as definite characteristic features of a playing technique. By so doing, the way is opened to examine detachedly the structural designs and resonance factors resulting from keyboard idioms and patterns. The orchestrator's task in working with this source material calls for idiomatic conversion of musical values of one medium to those of another, without the loss of pertinent details or musical style.

The *Reference Chart of Keyboard Idioms and Patterns,* as employed herein, has been designed to recognize and facilitate, by a systematic and specialized study plan, the orchestral adaptation of keyboard music's most common stylistic technicalities. Each entry of the *Reference Chart* represents a specific detail of a playing technique. Its idiomatic setting for orchestral instruments can constitute it as a model for all subsequent repetitions. Each category in the *Reference Chart* is kept in context whenever structural elements are directly affected by their inclusion.

The study plan, as outlined, is intended to stimulate creative thinking, for orchestration deals with multiple voice parts in kaleidoscopic combinations of mixed colors, strengths, and intensities. As most of the examples are projected through scorings for strings, wood-winds, brasses, and full orchestra, the transformations can be not only observed, but evaluated, appraised, and applied to meet scoring requirements. (Similar methodology is used in the author's book, "Band Scoring, A Comprehensive Manual.")

The practicality of this text has been considered from a conductor's point of view as well as from that of a composer. Its emphasis is directed toward the realization of the greatest possible effect with the least possible means. This duality of approach is intended to facilitate methods of procedure and to recognize the variable technical proficiency of orchestras.

Teaching experience over a period of many years at all levels provided the data for this text. It is because this experience showed conclusively the regularity of common errors dealing essentially with purely technical aspects of structural problems that equal proportions of textures and timbres have been incorporated as basic text materials.

Finally, in recognition of the exigencies of time, a *Workbook* has been prepared which includes numerous examples of scoring, with direct reference and relationship to all the entries contained in the *Reference Chart of Keyboard Idioms and Patterns.* Satisfactory results can be expected if a systematic study-work plan is carried out with the models given in the *Workbook,* in conjunction with the detailed analysis and application of this text.

My sincere thanks and gratitude are acknowledged to Miss Helen Reichard and Prof. A. Kunrad Kvam of Douglass College (Rutgers University) and to Felix Greissle for their valued assistance and cooperation. A special note of thanks is also rendered to Nicolas Slonimsky for his scholarly suggestions, to Arthur Cohn for his expert reading of the final proofs, and to my wife for her untiring efforts in the preparation and proofreading of the manuscript.

Joseph Wagner

CONTENTS

KEY FOR NUMBERING EXAMPLES AND FIGURES

I	Introductory Chapters 1 to 9
S	Chapter 10 for strings
W	Chapters 11 to 16 for wood-winds
B	Chapters 17 to 26 for brass
P	Chapters 27 to 32 for percussion
H	Chapter 33 for harp
C	Chapter 33 for celesta
Or	Chapter 33 for organ
O	for remaining Chapters for full orchestra

ABBREVIATIONS FOR INSTRUMENTS

B. Cl.	Bass clarinet
B. D.	Bass drum
Bsns.	Bassoons
Cbs.	Contrabasses
Cbsns.	Contrabassoons
Cel.	Celesta
Cls.	Clarinets
Cors.	Cornets
Cym.	Cymbals
E. H.	English horn
Fl.	Flute
Hns.	Horns
Obs.	Oboes
Perc.	Percussion
Picc.	Piccolo
S. D.	Snare drum
Tamb.	Tambourine
Timp.	Timpani
Tpts.	Trumpets
Trbs.	Trombones
Tri.	Triangle
Vlas.	Violas
Vlcs.	Violoncellos
Vlns.	Violins
W. W.	Wood-winds

Chapter 1

MUSIC AS A GUIDE

> *Definition of Orchestration*
> *Origins of the Orchestra*
> *Orchestral Thinking*
> *Musical Structures and*
>   *Textures*

The dictionary defines an orchestra as "a band of musicians" and an orchestration as "an arrangement of music for an orchestra." These definitions, although general in character, serve the purpose reasonably well, except in the case of the term "orchestra." An ambiguity of definition arises from the fact that a concert or military band may also be regarded as "a band of musicians." How, then do they differ, and why is a distinction deemed necessary? Both groups have varying numbers of wood-wind, brass, and percussion instruments. The answer lies in the fundamental difference of the orchestra having a complete string choir as its principal section, around which all other sections are semidependent and adjusted. The string choir is the very core of orchestral thinking and writing.

A period of approximately one hundred years was required for the instrumentation of the symphony orchestra to become more or less standardized. Yet, from its very inception, the orchestra, devoted to the performance of symphonic music and its counterparts, the oratorio and the opera, has relied on the string choir for its maximum effort and effect. To a large degree, the development and continuous progress of orchestration was made possible because of the flexibility, adaptability, and variety inherently idiomatic in the string section. It is a complete and independent section which, by its very nature, allows for a wide range of adaptation and usefulness.

Music scored for the string choir, idiomatically and with proper regard for harmonic structural considerations, will provide an excellent foundation for orchestration in any form. This point may be further emphasized in connection with the place held by the string section in the

1

orchestral repertory of pre-Bach composers. Their scores, for the most part written primarily for string orchestra with occasional added winds, remain active on concert programs not only because of their varying qualities as music but because of their excellent, idiomatic string writing. These early composers knew and understood the capacities of the string section remarkably well, as a study of Vivaldi's *The Seasons* will reveal.

Orchestration, defined as "an arrangement of music for an orchestra," is actually a highly specialized component of musical composition. It calls for a thorough working knowledge of theoretical music subjects (harmony, counterpoint, form, etc.) and an equally comprehensive understanding of the characteristics and peculiarities of all the various instruments employed in the contemporary symphony orchestra. Such matters as tonal range, technical capacities, combination possibilities, as well as the various tonal limitations, strengths, and weaknesses of each instrument, form an essential part of every orchestrator's technique. This kind of technique can be acquired in exactly the same way that facility in playing an instrument or composing becomes possible and practical —through the actual doing.

Students of orchestration need not be unduly concerned about their lack of playing experience of orchestral instruments. This limitation is not in itself a serious handicap, as can be shown by the achievements of two of the greatest innovators in this field, Hector Berlioz and Richard Wagner. Neither was proficient as an instrumental performer. Yet these two giants of orchestration managed to give their works the stamp of genius and originality. No, their excellence did not come from actual playing technique; rather, it was a result of their mastery and exploitation of all that had been done before them by composers of many styles and periods, plus a genius-size portion of musical intuition. This deduction is especially true in the case of Hector Berlioz. His extraordinary, epoch-making *Treatise on Instrumentation* shows most conclusively how he had not only mastered the technical matters of his craft, but had assimilated the very essence and spirit of the works he chose to examine and analyze.

The case of Richard Wagner is somewhat different, for here we find a composer who had little formal music education. He relied essentially upon a fantastic sense of musical intuition, but also learned his instrumental vocabulary, as did Berlioz, to a large degree, through his work as an orchestral conductor. Both of these titans owe a special debt of gratitude to Carl Maria von Weber, since his innovations led the way toward a new kind of orchestral thinking. To stress this point of thinking orchestrally is to start on the right road to orchestration, for to think orchestrally is to think *idiomatically*.

Before leaving this subject of thinking orchestrally, we should take into consideration the fact that while great composers all follow a common musical instinct, their pathways in art may diverge widely. Robert Schumann's orchestral works have been assailed by some music critics and conductors as being unorchestral. This same criticism has also been directed toward the purely orchestral portions of the Chopin works for piano and orchestra. In the case of the latter, the weakness and ineffectiveness of the orchestration are more apparent and unfortunate. The orchestral writing of both composers reflects, in varying degrees, their preoccupation with music frequently conceived in terms of the piano. This musical inclination is reflected in the texture of the music— its construction, thematic ideas, figurations, and harmonic spacings.

To think orchestrally is to conceive and hear all the instruments of the orchestra idiomatically and to further understand their technical and tonal values along with their over-all potentials. The acquisition of such mastery in orchestration is not incompatible with distinction in other mediums of musical expression. The orchestral works of both Debussy and Ravel are not only beautifully conceived and scored but are also epoch-making in their sonorities and textures; at the same time, their piano compositions are gems of pianistic technique and expression. This dual kind of musical personality may also be applied to both Brahms and Strauss, inasmuch as their vocal compositions constitute a significant part of the song repertory; likewise, both composers' orchestral works are firmly entrenched in the symphonic repertory and are likely to remain so for many generations to come. In the case of Brahms we find a highly individualistic style of scoring based on well-established procedures of the more conservative type, while the works of Strauss are the exact antithesis: they are bold and sensational in their sheer instrumental virtuosity.

From these comparisons the student will discover the wisdom of acquiring the understanding of idiomatic orchestral values along with the free play of musical intuition as the first step toward a flexible scoring technique. This knowledge, once gained and assimilated, may be enhanced by combining it with the advantages received from all the subjects studied in the related field of musical history.

The art of scoring for orchestra is by no means a static or rule-bound process. Frequently there will be several possible ways to score a given piece, each quite different in specific plan and sound, yet each quite acceptable in its ultimate effect. Such differences, occurring from the choice of timbres (tonal colors) rather than changes of structure, may conceivably be considered as matters of personal preference. However, changes made in such technicalities as melody placement, harmony positions, or rhythmic fidelity may occasion distortions beyond the limits intended by the composer. Further study will clarify the need for considerable attention to the matters of style, form, and construction, which have to be thoroughly appraised before actual scoring can be started. The following sections have been designed to coordinate the technical details of the compositional aspects of orchestration.

Chapter 2

COMPOSITION AND ORCHESTRATION STYLES

Musical Values
Style Evolutions
Composing Techniques versus
Orchestration

The first consideration in planning an orchestral score should be of purely musical values. What is the style of the music? Is it *homophonic*[1] or *polyphonic?*[2] Are its stylistic patterns characteristic of a specific period? What is its harmonic texture? When these characteristics have been properly judged, actual planning of the score can start. It should be remembered that each period of music, from the Baroque to the Modern, has rather definite, identifying mannerisms which offer specific aid in deciding upon the *instrumentation* (instruments used) which is in keeping with these characteristics. In orchestral transcriptions, the student would do well either to refer to original scores by the composer or, if such scores are not available, to make comparative studies of scores by other contemporary composers. A mixture of stylistic patterns in music is just as undesirable as a faulty combination of melody, rhythm, and harmony. The essentials of the music should not be changed from the original when orchestrating.

For more than two hundred years, composers of orchestral music have constantly sought to expand the potentials of all the instruments at their disposal, just as they sought to experiment with the basic elements of their craft. This predisposition toward experimentation in the matter of orchestration has, in many cases, brought about personal scoring techniques which have become identifying trademarks as much as the personal mannerisms in their compositions.

[1] A harmonized melody.
[2] Two or more independent parts without harmonization.

5

To clarify this point further, one has only to compare four representative symphonies—covering a span of a little more than one century—
with differing instrumentations. The following scores are recommended
for this survey: Schubert No. 5, Beethoven No. 5, Tchaikovsky No. 5, and
Shostakovitch No. 5. The instrumentation of the Schubert score has less
than the minimum usually associated with the Classic period, while the
Shostakovitch score has a maximum one—quite regular for twentieth-
century scores in this form. The two middle scores, Beethoven and
Tchaikovsky, become increasingly instructive when consideration is given
to their identical instrumentation.

First, note the gradually increased number of wind instruments and
their progressive importance, both melodically and harmonically. Then
observe the writing for the brass, especially the horns and trumpets.
Follow these parts in their gradual release from the scale limitations of
natural horns and trumpets (valveless) to their later melodic freedom
and flexibility resulting from the adoption of valve instruments. Notice
that the percussion section, with the exception of the timpani, is conspicuously absent until the Shostakovitch score. Attention should also
be directed to the changing details of phrasing, *tessituras,*[1] and balance.

These observations apply only to instrumental considerations. They
do not evaluate the extraordinary development of compositional and
orchestral styles present in these symphonies. This dramatic evolution
(not revolution) is best observed by a comparison of the two extremes—
the Schubert and Shostakovitch scores.

In the Schubert symphony, the texture rarely deviates from the real
parts of three- or four-voice harmonic spellings. There is a minimum of
doublings and infrequent use of added fillers—hence a limited degree of
sonority. The orchestration is pure, transparent, lucid—in keeping with
the emotional level of the music.

The Shostakovitch score reveals the extent of developments in compositional techniques and orchestral thinking. Here we find frequent
doublings and fillers along with sustained harmony parts. The composer
seeks out the flavor and pungency of orchestral effects for their sheer
coloristic values. Extremes of instrumental ranges are exploited, as are
totally different spacing arrangements. Increased emphasis is given to
each section of the orchestra as a complete and/or semi-independent
unit, sometimes referred to as "individualized choirs." These combined
factors contribute greatly to this score's greater sonority, tonal strength,
and intensity.

A feeling of appropriateness pervades the pages of these four symphonies. They carry the conviction that the thematic and harmonic

---

[1] The range covered by any given part.

materials were conceived for the exact orchestration as given and that any other scoring would have been unsuitable and ineffectual.

The quality of music and its orchestration do not depend upon the amount of its sonority or artificial brilliance. There are times when a two-voiced contrapuntal line has far greater power and drive than the loudest *tutti*.[1] These things are a matter of good musical taste and style and should be treated as such.

The importance of style in orchestration may be seen by evaluating the scores of two composers with opposing temperaments. For this purpose, the overtures *Anacreon* by Luigi Cherubini (1760–1842) and the *Roman Carnival* by Hector Berlioz (1803—1869) will serve as excellent models. In the Cherubini work the instrumentation differs only slightly from that employed by Berlioz. The differences are in the latter's use of a piccolo, an English horn, and a percussion section. Why, then, do these overtures differ so greatly in their total effect and sonority?

The answer lies primarily in the compositional techniques of the two composers, for their styles have little in common. Cherubini, the Classicist, steeped in the tradition of the conventions and formalities of the past, was always mindful of his servant, *counterpoint*. The then rising tide of Romanticism touched him but slightly and he remained constant to his conservative Classic concepts. Berlioz, on the other hand, was extravagant, daring, and explosive, with a natural inclination toward pioneering—the incarnate antithesis of conservatism. His whole concept of music making was given over to the new-found freedoms and excesses then sweeping the artistic world. He used the orchestra as a medium for the projection of his vivid, imaginative ideas—a well-nigh perfect blending of the compositional-orchestrational technique.

An interesting experiment, emphasizing these points of view, may be obtained by playing these two overtures on the piano. While *Anacreon* sounds convincing as abstract music, the *Roman Carnival* becomes surprisingly pale and colorless when divorced from its orchestral setting. Generally, this piano-playing test serves very well to illustrate the contention that the most successful orchestral scores lose their complete coloristic identification when considered apart from their original orchestral settings.

[1] Passage for full orchestra.

Chapter 3

TEXTURES AND TECHNIQUES

Thinking Orchestrally
Practical Instrumentation
   Considerations
Comparative Studies of
   Techniques and Textures
Appropriateness in
   Orchestration
Operatic Influences

Rimsky-Korsakov has been credited with the assertion that "orchestration *is* composition." This truism emphasizes the importance of thinking orchestrally when composing for orchestra. Orchestration is not a subject that can be mastered by textbook study only. It requires infinite curiosity about what has been done and what is being done by writers of orchestral music at all periods. Textbook study and application serve as a guide in stimulating purposeful thinking and offer sound advice on all practical and technical matters. It is for the student to put these elements into practice by following the procedures which will help the eyes to hear, for, after all, notes are not sounds but symbols for sounds. One suggestion in this direction is to acquire a good score-reading technique. Following a score with recordings or with "live" performances can be helpful in this respect, as all visual parts then become identified with orchestral sound. Familiarity with the reading of all clefs and transpositions[1] in current use is indispensable.

Unnecessary awkwardness caused by inherently unidiomatic writing is to be avoided. Many student attempts, though meritorious in many ways, are often killed by passages which simply cannot be played with any degree of technical perfection. Other passages may look intriguing on paper but fail to "come off" or "sound." Such passages can be corrected only by forming good habits of orchestral thinking. A playable score is usually indicative of music with artistic merit.

[1] The writing of parts higher or lower than the actual sound.

In planning the orchestration of piano music, it is desirable to recognize and evaluate the personal style, mannerisms, and period of each composer. By way of illustration, examine the symphonic works of Mozart and Schubert. Two suggested scores for this purpose are Mozart's Symphony No. 35 (*Haffner*), and the great Schubert C major Symphony No. 7.

Mozart employs a typical Classical instrumentation: wood-winds, horns, trumpets, and timpani in pairs, along with the usual strings. The clarinets were added by the composer in a final revision of the work. A survey of the forty-one symphonies by Mozart reveals irregular numbers of wind instruments, with no apparent attempt to standardize the instrumentation. He simply scored his symphonic works for those instruments which were available. (This concept of practicality has returned to twentieth-century orchestration.) The trombones were not included in a single Mozart symphony! The style is a masterful blending of homophonic and polyphonic textures, the latter having frequent short canonic imitations and *fugatos*.[1] The part writing rarely exceeds the usual four parts except when *tuttis* call for a limited use of doublings and fillers. (Doublings are to be regarded as added voices in unisons or octaves, while fillers are extra harmony notes added in either the medium or high registers.)

Mozart's orchestration possesses an elusive quality of delicate transparency which distinguishes it as being among the finest examples of clear musical thinking. This transparency results from textures of real parts with few extraneous notes. Melodic outlining or unison doubling and sustained fillers are practically nonexistent. All musical values are purely and clearly stated with not only adequate scoring, but often with a delightfully tantalizing interplay of timbres revealing a craftsmanship of sheer genius. The extraordinary thing is that Mozart's dynamic levels of *forte*-to-*piano* are seldom exceeded in any of his symphonic works!

Yet these scores, which appear to be quite simple technically, are decidedly hazardous—especially for amateur orchestras. What lies behind this apparent contradiction? The characteristic of transparency, more than any other single factor, provides the clue—for music of this texture requires technical perfection for a first-class performance. Difficulties (in Mozart) are not the result of awkward part writing. Quite the contrary. It is because all parts are written with such clarity, taste, and finesse that these scores require purity of sound, style, and sure technical control from each player to do them justice. Each instrument is allowed its full play of expressiveness, strength, and range without relying on sustained parts or doublings for its total effectiveness. Weak

[1] A passage or movement in fugal style.

ranges of the wood-winds are not engulfed by sustained harmony parts in the same compass that would cover up any true solo character and rob a passage of its clarity and definition.

In the case of the Schubert symphony, there is considerable expansion and development of the instrumental resources as compared to the Mozart opus. Schubert's wind and timpani grouping remains conventional, but the writing for the brass—especially the horns and trombones —is advanced beyond that of traditional Classic usage. This change in instrumentation, however, does not in itself account for the difference in sonority of these works. Schubert's music is, for the most part, homophonically conceived, formalized counterpoint being relatively rare. A second point in texture variance may be noted by comparing the number of voice parts employed by each composer. Schubert frequently wrote unison and octave doublings along with fillers to extend the melodic and harmonic ranges for greater sonorities. His scoring technique gives further evidence of change and variance, as can be noted primarily in the importance given to the melodic line, with its greater dependence upon harmonizations. Because of the greater prominence given to the harmony, observe how the heavier instruments, horns and trombones, are assigned to these parts. Naturally, a fuller sonority is achieved by this method of scoring, and the degree of transparency retained is in proportion to the number and kind of sustaining parts.

Transparency is not the predominating characteristic of Schubert's music, yet a degree of this quality is present when the texture is essentially in four-part writing and without many sustaining voices or doubled parts. It should also be noted that modulation plays a more important part in Schubert's harmonic patterns, along with a prevailing use of the principal triads, which is another characteristic of the late Classic period. Elementary rhythmic patterns likewise assume more importance with this composer, for this kind of natural momentum builds climaxes and increases emotional tension. In summation, it can be established that the fundamental items of texture and style, as analyzed in the Schubert score, provide the roots of change which were to be fully explored and developed by the composers of the later Romantic period.

Before leaving the study of the scores under consideration, a further examination based on the use of the brass instruments should be helpful. In both scores the horns and trumpets rarely have extended melodic lines, being used primarily for sustaining harmony parts or building climaxes in simple harmonizations. In this connection both composers wrote for the natural horns and trumpets—without valves or pistons—and therefore were limited in over-all scale tones. Nevertheless, Schubert managed occasional melodic and harmonic prominence for the horns beyond the limits usual for his time. His trumpet parts likewise have greater independence from couplings with the horns than those in the Mozart score. However, their individual compositional styles furnish the real clue to their divergent techniques of orchestration.

It is of interest to note that melodic lines for horns and trumpets, when they do occur, are usually confined to the tones of the principal triads. This limitation is also applicable to broken chords and fanfares, since these passages were particularly effective in building climaxes in cadences. Quite likely these very limitations of available scale tones for horns, and particularly trumpets, had much to do with the compositional thinking of the composers of the Classic and early Romantic periods, as this factor forced them to derive much of their melodic material from the principal triad combinations. From Haydn to Beethoven and Brahms, there is a predominance of this kind of melodic thinking that was so frequent and regular that it can hardly be considered as simply a personal preference or mannerism.

The orchestra of the symphonic world of music represents but half the total development of this highly specialized medium. Another vital and less formalized division of music was steadily moving forward, with notable results. The ever-expanding horizon of opera offered challenging opportunities with different concepts and possibilities. In its beginnings, the opera orchestra did little more than accompany; but with gradual development and growth came greater freedom, independence, and importance. The opera orchestra became a complementary and contributing factor, a coordinating medium. As the composer of successful opera must be concerned with character delineation in the projection of his music, so too must his orchestra assist in defining such characterization. The opera scores of Gluck and Mozart led the way in establishing the orchestra as an additional unit of dramatic support. The Romantic genius of Weber, notably in his opera, *Der Freischütz,* created a totally new and startling conception by using the orchestra as a contributing means as well as a supporting unit of independent power and force. His orchestration not only delineated, but also created and sustained descriptive moods as indicated by the libretto.

Especially notable was Weber's imaginative use of the wind instruments. In this respect he followed the lines set by his most illustrious predecessors in developing and exploiting the full potentialities of these instruments. This was a further step toward the recognition and realization of musical composition being inseparably woven into the imaginative qualities of orchestra sonorities. The grandiose operatic scores of the two Richards—Wagner and Strauss—continued the expansion of these ideas with virtuoso techniques which culminated orchestral developments for the nineteenth century.

Chapter 4

INSTRUMENTAL CONSIDERATIONS

The previous brief historical survey of orchestration can now be correlated with more specific details of scoring. In Chap. 1, importance of the music, as such, was emphasized; in this chapter, importance of the instruments will be considered. Previously it was established that the string choir is the very foundation of the orchestra. This section, because of its more or less fixed timbres, is a homogeneous grouping, notwithstanding its wide range of possible effects and expressive powers. Varieties of contrast and expression lie in the methods of application—the ways in which the section is used melodically, harmonically, and rhythmically.

Inconsistencies in
  Standardization
Musical Values in
  Orchestration
An Analogy of the Visual
  Arts and Orchestration
Definition by Timbres

Standardization of this kind is impossible if applied to the other three sections of the orchestra: wood-wind, brass, and percussion. One has only to hear a single, identical note played on a flute and an oboe to recognize the lack of fixed timbres in the wood-wind choir. Similar timbre differences exist within the brass and percussion sections. Yet there are certain areas of timbre similarities; due to divisions in the sections, that will be discussed in detail at a later time. Suffice it to say now that each wind instrument has a definite, characteristic tonal color—a fact which establishes a unique paradox. Although a great variety of tonal colors and strengths is possible with judicious use of these instruments, a continued, unvaried playing of any single one of them, especially on a melodic line, can produce an unnecessary monotony. This is why the sensitive orchestrator plans his scores so as to give a variable interplay of timbres, both melodically and harmonically. In addition, the matters

12

of range, tonal spread, and *tessitura* must be given serious consideration and study since all the wind instruments have strong and weak ranges, as well as peculiarities of timbre that affect their blending possibilities.

It has been said that an experienced orchestra conductor can judge the quality of a score by the distribution of parts in a *forte tutti.* Why should such a test be a criterion of quality? The answer lies in the manner of chord distribution. Which instruments play which chord tones and in what *tessitura?* Note well: The combination of timbre, *tessitura,* and dynamics are the three elements that require constant evaluation if a balanced sonority is to be achieved. The necessity for profiles of balance is present for every measure of orchestration regardless of styles, textures, or ranges.

Obviously, the volume in a *forte* passage for a flute will not be the same as that of a horn or a trumpet, any more than a *forte* stroke on the triangle will approximate the same dynamic as a crash with a pair of cymbals. It follows then that all dynamics are comparative. Individual experimentation along these lines would not only be enlightening, but helpful, in evaluating relative timbres, sonorities, and capacities. Numerous miscalculations of comparative tonal strengths, within a specific dynamic range, can be detected in many scores by Classic composers. Felix Weingartner's book *On the Performance of Beethoven's Symphonies* contains pertinent references to representative errors of balance and clarity and gives definite recommendations for their correction.

Problems of voice distribution become still more acute in dealing with the instruments of the brass choir. There is a marked difference in the tonal strength and timbre of a horn and a trumpet playing the same note with the same dynamic. This comparison could also include the trombone, with reservations. Because these tonal differences exist in varying degrees, detailed study and analysis will be devoted to these problems in connection with the full examination of these instruments as separate choirs.

From the comparative studies made thus far, there can be little doubt that the approach to music from the Classic period will be inconsistent with music from either the Romantic or Modern periods. In orchestrating a movement from a Mozart piano sonata, one would use an instrumentation which would be quite inappropriate for an orchestration of representative music by Liszt or Tchaikovsky. And the instrumentation would not be the sole point of difference. The complete approach, the manner and idiomatic use of the instruments, would likewise be on a totally different plane. Harp *glissandos,* blaring trumpets, shrieking horns, and explosions from the battery (percussion section), all have their rightful place in the over-all scheme of orchestral writing but cannot be condoned in music far removed in time from the natural niche allotted to these particular modern innovations.

Before proceeding with the actual detailed study of all the instruments, the following analogy is suggested as a means of obtaining a new and useful perspective: Orchestration has many points in common with the visual arts. There are the obvious elements of design, color, and movement. But there is another major common denominator which forms a more basic connection as a starting point for reasonable comparisons.

It will be generally agreed that in painting and photography the illusion of a foreground and background is ever present. This same illusionary characteristic can also be found in music. In the artistic representation of the visual dimensions, whether it be photographic or on canvas, the projection of this natural precept of comparative proximity has become a required element for normal comprehension. Everyone's daily existence depends upon the individual's ability to make this constant distinction between foreground and background. The ear must also make similar analysis with any combination of sounds in motion. Woe to the person who does not recognize the difference between the siren of the police patrol car and a boy's competing police whistle! Here is a specific example of timbre recognition.

The painter achieves a two-dimensional effect of foreground and background by means of color contrasts and composition. The orchestrator must accomplish the same illusion by means of contrasting timbres, along with the right balancing of these sonorities. Occasionally these two elements, foreground and background, merge with such subtle craftsmanship that only the trained eye and ear can detect the points of contact. When this joining process is skillfully carried out, the result is a smooth, naturally flowing line and texture. The connection between painting and music is further emphasized by noting the number of composers who have received direct inspiration from this sympathetic union. (Walton's *Portsmouth Point* and Rachmaninov's *Isle of the Dead* serve as good examples.)

If painting without an intelligible definition of foreground and background is comparatively meaningless, imagine an orchestral score without tonal definition. Such a score would degenerate into a hopelessly chaotic jumble of scrambled sounds. The orchestrator's task is to organize his score so that performance will reveal clarity of the leading melodic ideas, with secondary parts adjusted according to their relative importance. When this is done with sureness and subtlety, a natural feeling of a musical foreground and background will exist.

The trick here is to accomplish these things without any impression of artificiality. The experienced orchestrator knows that the leading melodic ideas must be assigned to instruments with sufficient carrying strength; he knows that the choice of such instruments depends upon the *tessitura* of the complete part; he knows that the harmonic scheme, serving as a background, must be properly spaced and assigned to instruments with contrasting timbres; and he also knows that a needless clash of melodic and harmonic lines kills the fluidity of the leading ideas. His experience has proved beyond a doubt that foreground elements cannot become obscured by background elements of secondary counterpoints or by harmonic and rhythmic patterns. He further understands the value of being able to fuse his foreground and background components with ease and surety.

All these assets are the means by which a serviceable working technique can be realized. Likewise, the student composer must make them a part of his daily creative life. If "orchestration is composition," then compositional thinking and idiomatic scoring become synonymous. Musical thinking of this order will facilitate and establish a subconscious habit of hearing all varieties and shades of sound through the inner ear. The creative process thus becomes stimulated and, with effort, can be directed toward matters of style, form, and texture.

As with most generalities, suggestions, and rules, exceptions often occur which result from highly specialized considerations based upon the imaginative urgings of the unusual. One has only to see a few of the many Monet canvases of the same cathedral painted at various hours of the day, and thereby reflecting a seemingly endless variety of light and shade, to appreciate the relationship of changing values in art. The arts, in any form, are not static. They must inevitably move through periods of evolution in order to survive. Their shape and substance are in the eyes—and the ears—of the beholder. Monet, and his French colleagues of the Impressionist movement, created a highly imaginative approach to painting by merging the foreground-background concept with its ensuing moods of hazy, veiled reminiscence. Composers followed in the path of the painters but, as always, the Gallic intuitive feeling for clarity of definition prevailed. Debussy and Ravel assumed the role of musical French Impressionists . . . and a new style of orchestration was born. Yet the combined scores of these innovators rarely abandon the musical conception of foreground and background. A notable exception in this case may be observed in the Introduction of Ravel's *La Valse*. Here the programmatic idea calls for a mood of confused sounds from which the "birth of the valse" emerges. The final measures of this work are intentionally replete with chaotic sounds, again in keeping with the depiction of the collapse of a golden age. Orchestral effects in this category prove their validity by establishing and maintaining both pictorial and emotional moods.

Thus, the composer achieves through sound what the painter does through pigments. In this connection, it should be observed that purely orchestral effects—in all shades of colorings—should be reserved for music of mood, be it opera, ballet, or program music. When such effects are incorporated in abstract music, the results are apt to sound artificial and inappropriate. This is an area in which the orchestrator must rely on the precepts of good taste. The dividing line is naturally influenced somewhat by the qualities of design and construction. Conversely, program music is rarely successful without imaginative scoring kept within reasonable limits. Realism, when overextended, goes beyond the tenets of good art in music.

As music comes into being by means of ordered sounds in motion, whether it be a simple homophonic piece or a more complicated contrapuntal texture, the orchestrator must be ever mindful to avoid scoring plans which might obscure the clarity of all the interdependent elements. This admonition is an important factor in the study of the visual-art–music analogy; for music, like painting, is not necessarily confined to a single foreground idea but may have several semimajor themes sounding simultaneously. Most music, contrapuntally conceived, is in this category. As a fugue, with its sundry adaptations, is composed of a principal subject in conjunction with secondary counterpoints, it follows logically that orchestration of this form be scored with appropriate clarity and definition. Consider a performance of a fugue for piano, played without profile of the primary and secondary thematic parts. Such a performance would be a meaningless jumble of notes, unworthy of attention or consideration. Orchestration carried out with a similar negative disregard for musical values would become hopelessly chaotic. Thematic definition can be achieved only when tonal strengths and timbre contrasts are in balance with melodic *tessituras* and harmonic spacings which allow unhampered movement of each separate part.

Definition by timbres and its dependent area of clarity are problems resulting from the combining of several unequal melodic ideas—that is, a main theme in conjunction with a counter melody, rhythmic figuration, or *ostinato*.[1] Passages in this category must include consideration of tonal strengths or weights in addition to timbres. There is also the unavoidable problem of range differentials in the extreme high and low compasses, especially with the wood-winds. However, the identifying timbre and tonal strength of each wind instrument, whether alone or in combination, provides an almost limitless scope for thematic materials which may vary in importance. Similarly, secondary accompanying parts of harmonic and rhythmic patterns can be adjusted so that they will not interfere with the clarity of the principal motives.

[1] Continuously repeated phrase or figuration.

A specific example of this idea may be found in the Farandole from the *L'Arlésienne* Suite No. 2 by Bizet.[1] Here, the two main themes of contrasting character are exposed at the beginning of the dance without distraction from the secondary parts. Then these two themes are deftly combined, adding rhythmic counterparts with perfect clarity. The bolder of the two themes is always placed in the brass while the skipping dance tune, used as a counterpoint, never leaves the upper wood-winds and strings. Although the scoring-on-paper of the latter groups may appear to be unduly strong because of the doubled parts, they will not overpower the brass instruments which are playing in their best *tessituras*. This represents a beginning toward the study and recognition of the differences in instrumental timbres and tonal strengths and their importance.

The scope of orchestrational possibilities appears to be limitless even after two hundred years of experimentation. The orchestral works of Haydn and Mozart differ greatly from those of Schumann and Brahms, while those of Liszt and Wagner are equally distant from those of Hindemith and Stravinsky. Note well: It is not just a matter of compositional differences; rather it is an awareness of instrumental idiomatic capacities and their effect upon the composer's musical horizons. This thought may be realized in detail through a comparative analysis of Mozart's Symphony No. 35 (K. 385) and the Prokofiev *Classical Symphony*, Op. 25. In commenting on the latter score, the Russian composer and critic Boris Asafiev says, "The composer's idea in writing this work was to catch the spirit of Mozart, and to put down that which, if he were living now, Mozart might put into his scores." Both symphonies achieve their respective ends with a similar minimum of means; both require the same Classical instrumentation and both have a polished sophistication. It is in the matters of harmony, instrumental brilliance, and virtuosity that one finds the greatest differences in the two works. Mozart was always himself, whereas critics have speculated that Prokofiev may have had "his tongue in his cheek" when writing this opus.

[1] According to Nicolas Slonimsky, this suite was orchestrated by Guiraud after Bizet's death.

Chapter 5

INSTRUMENTS OF THE ORCHESTRA

The instruments of the orchestra are grouped in families according to their timbre and means of tone production. Intersectional divisions occur in the wood-winds because of three distinct timbre

Divisions
Importance of the
Harmonic Series
Spacings and Balance

qualities: non-reeds, single reeds, and double reeds. The brass instruments form a single unit notwithstanding their somewhat dissimilar tonal characteristics.

The family groupings have, in many instances, the advantage of inter-divisions which permit four-part writing within a single timbre. Each grouping collectively has a tonal compass comparable to the four basic ranges of the human voice: soprano, alto, tenor, and bass. The five sectional groupings for orchestration appear as follows:

1. STRINGS (high to low)
   Violin, viola, violoncello, contrabass (double bass and/or bass)
2. WOOD-WINDS (high to low)
   Non-reeds: Piccolo, flute, alto flute, bass flute
   Single Reeds: Clarinets—E♭, alto, bass
                Saxophones—soprano, alto, tenor, baritone, bass
   Double Reeds: Oboe, English horn, bassoon, contrabassoon
3. BRASS
   Horn, trumpet, cornet, trombone, tuba
4. TIMPANI and PERCUSSION
5. SUPPLEMENTARY INSTRUMENTS WITHOUT SECTIONAL DESIGNATION
   Harp, celesta, piano, organ

18

Combined in an actual score they will appear as follows:

Rimsky-Korsakov
Capriccio Espagnol, Op. 34

The general plan of this handbook, for combining these instruments in score form, is based upon a system of doublings and fillers that arise from spacings found in the natural harmonic series, in addition to the accepted practices used in four-part harmonizations. The following chart is a working guide for the various classifications.

Soprano	**Alto**
Piccolo	Clarinet (1st)
Flute	English horn
Oboe	Saxophone (alto)
Clarinet (E♭)	Trumpet (2nd)
Saxophone (soprano)	Horn (1st and 3rd)
Trumpet (1st)	Trombone (1st)
Violin (1st)	Violin (2nd)

Tenor	**Bass**
Clarinet (2nd)	Bass clarinet
Clarinet (alto)	Bassoon
Saxophone (tenor)	Contrabassoon
Horn (2nd and 4th)	Saxophone (baritone)
Trombone (2nd)	Trombone (bass)
Viola	Tuba
	Cello
	Bass

This listing is not to be considered as the final word on the subject, since more exact divisional directions will be given in subsequent chapters. It does, nevertheless, represent the pattern of things to come in the matter of *range spreads* for doublings and fillers.

SPACINGS AND BALANCE

The proper interval spacing and balance of chord tones in an orchestral score may be achieved for all practical purposes by applying the lessons learned from the interval pattern of the natural harmonic series. No other single source material is of equal importance. The harmonic series for one-line C[1] is as follows:

[1] Two octaves below middle C.

Figure I-1

As an experiment, strike—*fortissimo*—one-line C on a piano with the damper pedal depressed. Then, press down silently any of the whole notes up to and including number 8. (The remaining higher tones are too weak to be picked up.) Release the key of the fundamental C along with the damper pedal. The selected note will continue to vibrate. The explanation lies in the fact that the overtones, now undampened, are allowed to vibrate freely. This phenomenon, multiplied many times over, accounts for the source of resonance for the piano and the harp with their sounding boards acting as resonators. Further experiments will reveal that the lower tones in the harmonic series ("Chord of Nature") will be stronger than the higher ones. **Note:** The quarter notes in the series are not exactly in pitch with the tempered scale and therefore will not sound. Closer study of this harmonic series will also reveal the complete lack of close-position chords in the bass clef, but a crowding of the overtones as the series ascends from middle C. Here, in this scale of nature, can be found the best pattern for doublings and fillers. Of the ten triad tones appearing in the series, there are five roots, three fifths, and two thirds. This proportion of triad tones will be generally acceptable in chordal progressions regardless of the number of added doublings and/or fillers.

There is one more lesson to be learned about the resonance factor of the piano that can be applied to the sonority problems of orchestration. Play—*forte*—the chord of C major, with middle C as the root, but *without* the damper pedal. Careful listening to the resonance of this chord shows that it has little or no vibrancy. Next, play the same chord, but with the damper pedal depressed. Observe the change in sonority. The sound is fuller, more vibrant, because the overtones of the full chord are free to vibrate, picking up the "sympathetic vibra-

Figure I-2

tions" from their fundamentals. Repeat this experiment using an expanded C major chord. Notice the increased resonance and vibrancy by the addition of three more voice parts and lower fundamentals. From these experiments it will be obvious that piano music receives its resonance in proportion to its tonal spread and that the vibrancy of its sonority is dependent upon the use of the damper pedal.

Figure I-3

At first glance these elementary experiments may seem to be over simplified and lacking any direct relationship to orchestration, but nothing could be farther from the truth. Actually, the connection between the piano and orchestra needs to be thoroughly assimilated, and for the following reason: There is no damper pedal in the orchestra; it must be built into each orchestration.

But how is the effect of the damper pedal to become an integral part of an orchestral score? The orchestra's equivalent of the piano's resonance may be realized through the use of effective spacing of all melodic and harmonic elements, along with the judicious arrangement of sustained harmony parts. Chord spacings similar to the following may be permissible for piano writing but they would be decidedly unidiomatic for orchestral instruments. Piano music is written so that it can be played by ten fingers. Orchestral music has an almost limitless number of voices to draw upon. The chords given in Fig. I-4 require further attention, but for a different reason. Notice that these chords have large note gaps in the middle register. (Compare spacings with the harmonic series.) In practical orchestration, such gaps would be highly undesirable, and only their complete rearrangement could bring about any semblance of tonal balance. Proceed on the premise that all notes sound as written and where written—no more, no less. Figure I-5 gives these chords, with the same number of voice parts, rearranged according to orchestral practices. Figures I-6 and I-7 are additional examples of chord spacings which should be studied and compared.

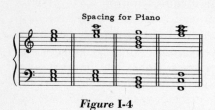

Figure I-4

Spacing for Piano

Spacing for Instruments

Figure I-5

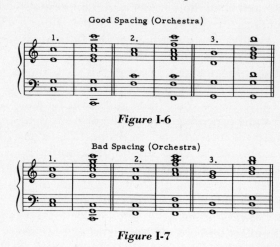

Good Spacing (Orchestra)

Figure I-6

Bad Spacing (Orchestra)

Figure I-7

From this survey of chord positions, it will be clear that good chord spacings are essential for balanced part writing. Doublings and fillers do not affect chord positions; rather they act as resonance factors. Doublings are to be considered as additional voice parts in unison with existing chord tones. Exceptions will be the addition of an octave to either a melody or a bass part, these being extensions in range.

Figure I-8

Figure I-9

Fillers, on the other hand, are to be regarded as added chord tones—notes not present in the original structure. They may be in any range and are to be considered as a means of extending the total range spread as well as of strengthening middle-range harmonic spacings.

Figure I-10

From these explanations it can be established that doublings tend to increase the volume, while fillers serve to give sonority and balance to the harmonic structure. Neither addition should affect chord positions. In general, harmonic textures, once established, should be maintained until each phrase or passage is completed. The octave bass part, given in Fig. I-10, is needed to support the range extension. **Caution:**

Remember that chord formations above the bass may be expanded without involving the positions of the chord progressions.

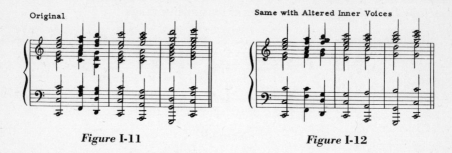

Figure I-11   *Figure* I-12

The applied principles, derived from the foregoing uses of doublings and fillers, may serve as preliminary models in any rearrangement of harmonic progressions.

SUMMARY OF DEDUCTIONS

1. Avoid close-position triads in fundamental positions or first inversions in the lower part of the bass range.

2. Added doublings and fillers sound best in this preferred order: octaves (unisons), fifths, and thirds.

3. In general, it is advisable to keep thirds, sevenths, and ninths out of the bass range when used as sustained harmony parts. Moving melodic lines or scales with these chord intervals are not included in this category.

4. Keep chord extensions, downward from middle C, in open position.

5. Arrange chord extensions, upward from middle C, in close position.

Chapter 6

THE STRING SECTION

Since the string section is a homogeneous grouping, not only in tonal color but in the manner of tone production as well, it is

Divisions
Tuning, Clefs, and Ranges
Group Practices

possible to consider its playing potentials collectively without any loss of pertinent data. Variation and intensity of tone color within the section result from each instrument's respective range and hence its vibrating characteristics. In this connection, it is to be noted that the outside strings (high and low) of each instrument have the greatest sonority and character, while the two middle ones are more neutral and less distinctive. Passages played in the higher positions on any of the strings acquire extra richness and vibrancy not otherwise obtainable.

The following chapters on string instruments, their playing techniques and coloristic devices, are sufficiently analyzed in conjunction with structural considerations to provide a serviceable foundation for practical scoring within a wide range of musical ideas and patterns. The instruments of this section include:

THE VIOLIN
Fr. *violon;* It. *violino;* Ger. *Violine*

THE VIOLA
Fr. *alto;* It. *viola;* Ger. *Bratsche*

THE VIOLONCELLO
Fr. *violoncelle;* It. *violoncello;* Ger. *Violoncell*

THE CONTRABASS
Fr. *contrebasse;* It. *contrabasso;* Ger. *Kontrabass*

Comprehensive Chart for Strings

TUNING, CLEFS, AND RANGES

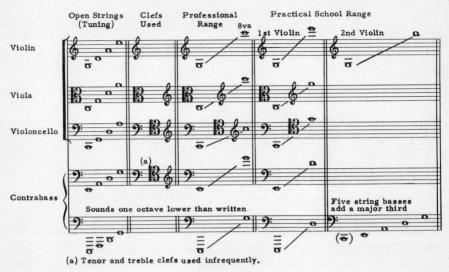

(a) Tenor and treble clefs used infrequently.

Figure I-13

Note. (Size Differences)

1. Violas are a perfect fifth lower than the violins.

2. Violoncellos are an octave lower than the violas.

3. Contra or double basses are an octave lower than the violoncellos and sound an octave lower than written. Hence, they are the only transposing instruments in the string choir. It is important to know that there are two types of contrabasses. The more common one is a four-string instrument, the lowest note of which is E, while those used in professional symphony orchestras usually have an added C string that lowers the range by a major third.

Note. (Clef Differences)

1. Violins use the treble clef only.

2. Violas use the alto and treble clefs.

3. Violoncellos normally use the bass clef and, for passages in the higher registers, the tenor and treble clefs.

4. Contrabasses rarely leave the bass clef, although some scores do have occasional parts in both the tenor and treble clefs.

Important. Clefs are changed only when it is a matter of practical convenience in avoiding excessive ledger lines. The following suggestions are given as a guide: (1) Avoid changing clefs for one or two notes. (2) Change clefs only when necessary and then at convenient breaks in the notation. (3) Remember that inexperienced string players usually are unfamiliar with clefs other than those commonly used.

STARTING POINT

In planning an orchestral score, it is always helpful to have some idea of the type and technical skill for which it is intended. Naturally, a score designed for a professional orchestra can have a greater scope of freedom in technical matters than one devised for amateur or school groups. Remember that violas in school and semiprofessional orchestras are apt to be the weakest part of the section. They will not have the same carrying power as the cellos—even in the same registers. In addition, all string parts which require advanced positions (starting a perfect fifth higher than the highest open strings) are difficult for inexperienced players of the average school orchestra.

GENERAL CONSIDERATIONS

1. Strings do not necessarily need to "breathe" as do the wood-winds and brasses, except for phrasing. However, any score which kept all the strings playing continuously would be dreary indeed.

2. Entrances of parts made after a silence of some duration add new interest, as each fresh attack focuses attention on the entering part. Therefore, planned occasional rests are valuable assets in relieving monotonous part writing. (Exception: For accompaniments of massed singing, disregard this suggestion and score for the full section throughout.)

3. Tempo markings (*Allegro, Largo,* etc., or their English equivalents) are placed at the top of the first page of a score in the upper left-hand corner. Subsequent changes of tempo are added at the top of the score directly over the measure of change.

4. All dynamics (*piano, forte,* etc., and such changes as *crescendo, diminuendo,* etc.) must be inserted in all affected parts. **Note:** Although tempo and dynamic directions in English would seem to be more practicable, experience shows that they are desirable only for music of rather restricted usage. Italian is the universally accepted language for music purposes.

5. Violoncello and contrabass parts should be written on two separate staves whenever possible. If they must be written on one staff, use double stems along with adequate rests to clearly indicate the correct notation for each instrument. If both instruments are to play the same notation on one staff, mark it *con bass.* If the notation is for cello only, add *senza bass.*

6. Use correct notation at all times. (Vocal and instrumental notations differ.)

7. Pay particular attention to all bow markings, so that they approximate the phrasing intended.

8. Do not resort to "8 va." unless absolutely necessary.

9. Accidentals occurring in divided parts must be repeated in each part affected by chromatic changes.

10. Divided string parts should be marked *divisi*. When unison playing is to be resumed, add *unis.*

Chapter 7

BOWING FOR ALL STRINGS

Bows for string instruments are made of a pliable wooden rod (back) with horsehairs (or gut threads) stretched from the bent

Basic Principles
Most Common Bowings
Special Bowings

head (point or tip) to a movable nut used for tightening. The hair part of the bow is drawn across the strings, thus setting them in vibration.

1. The term "bowing" has a twofold meaning. It refers to the continuous and alternating movement of the bow on the strings as well as to the markings that are used to indicate the direction of the bow. Thus, bow markings determine not only the manner in which the bow will be used but also the *style* (phrasing) of performance.

2. The degree or strength of tone depends, for the most part, on the amount of bow used, along with its placement and pressure on the strings. The string player divides the bow into three parts: the upper third near the tip, the middle, and the lower part near the frog or nut (heel).

These distinctions may have a practical application and understanding through the working out of the following experiment. (*a*) Balance a violin bow on the finger by finding its balancing center. Notice that this center is not the exact middle of the bow; the weight of the frog causes the balancing point to be a little toward the lower end. This experiment establishes the frog-end of the bow as its heaviest part. However, when string players place their bow on a string in playing position, they automatically center it. This playing center is used mostly for passages in the middle range of dynamics (*piano, mezzo-piano, mezzo-forte*). (*b*) Now, draw the bow over an edged surface. As the bow moves toward the frog (nut), notice that it is possible to exert considerable pressure on it. This lower third of the bow is best suited to the stronger dynamics (*forte, fortissimo,* etc.). It is ideal for sharp, dry, brittle parts that require strong accents with short bows. (*c*) Finally, draw the bow in the opposite direction toward the tip and observe that as the upper third of the

29

bow is reached, the amount of pressure decreases to practically zero. This upper third of the bow is usually reserved for all of the softer dynamics with little or no expressive overtones (*piano, pianissimo,* etc.). From this résumé, it is clear that the position of the bow on the string has considerable to do with the degree and variety of tone that will be produced. This simple explanation can be of definite value to non-string players who must struggle with bowings as an integral part of a scoring technique.

3. The amount of bow to be used for a given note, phrase, or passage is important in its relation to the placement of the bow. Naturally, notes of long duration require more bow than those of shorter duration. Yet, even this simple fact needs clarification, since tempos and dynamics must be considered as contributing factors. In this connection, the non-string player should be cognizant of differences in bow sizes used by the instruments of the section. Violoncello and contrabass bows are shorter than those used for the violins and violas and consequently require more frequent bow changes. This prevailing difficulty is particularly troublesome with inexperienced players where bow control is a major factor. The following signs are used as directional bow markings: down-bow ⊓; up-bow ∨.

Figure I-14

The importance of tempo in bowing may be examined in Fig. I-14. A long note of this type would be possible in two bows for most tempos up to a *moderate andante.* In faster tempos these four measures could be played in one bow, providing the dynamic is no stronger than *mezzo-forte.* If the same note is written *forte* or *fortissimo,* in any of the slow tempos, a bow for each measure would be desirable. In rapid tempos two bows, as given, would be satisfactory for the louder dynamic levels. In instances where long sustained notes or passages are involved, the orchestrator should be on the alert for entrances of important thematic material so that they may *start* with the proper bowings.

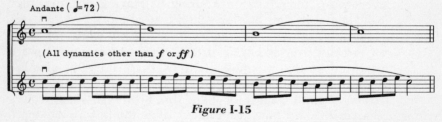

Figure I-15

An entirely different problem arises when passage work necessitates the shifting of the bow from one string to another, causing shifted finger positions. Passages in this category are difficult in proportion to the amount of bow shifting required and the size of intervals in the pattern.

Figure I-16

Caution. Long, sustained bows are difficult to control, as they require a first-class bow technique in order to maintain an even tone. Bowings which are combined with frequently shifting finger positions are equally troublesome because they need both bow control and finger dexterity.

4. Phrasing in string music is regulated by bow markings. It is common practice to have most new phrases start with a down-bow, although there are times when an up-bow will automatically mold a melody by a more natural balance and inflection, especially in the softer dynamic levels. Phrases which start with a *crescendo* and are followed by a *diminuendo* are in this category. The aim of all bowing is to achieve well-balanced phrases with natural inflections. Figure I-17 illustrates this point.

Figure I-17

a. Up-bows are idiomatic for all one-bow crescendos which start softly, as this brings the bow toward the frog (Example I-1a).

Example I-1a

b. Down-bows are normal for diminuendos that may start loudly and move toward a tonal fade-out. This bowing approaches the tip as the tone diminishes (Example I-1b).

Example I-1b

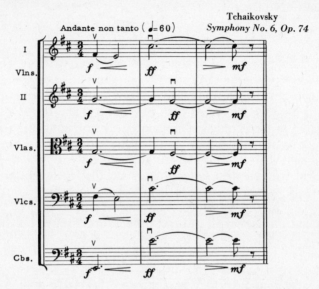

5. Almost any arrangement of short bows is technically easier than long bows in any form, although both styles are an integral part of a bowing technique. Short bows have the advantage of being adaptable to all speeds and dynamics whereas long bows are somewhat limited in their dynamic range. It is much less difficult to play a detached phrase with short, alternating bows than to play the same phrase with a single long bow.

6. Long slurs, as used for *legato* phrasing in piano music, are decidedly impractical if applied as bow markings. These slurs, sometimes extending over many measures, must of necessity be recast with bowings which will approximate the effect and style of the original phrase.

Example I-2

7. If no bow markings are indicated (⊓ or V), string players assume that alternate down-up bows are to be used. This is the least difficult of all bowings and is strictly non-*legato,* with each note receiving a fresh attack with each bow change. The specific kind of attack is dependent upon additional signs such as accents, *staccato* dots, and the various other symbols used for tonal definition.

Figure **I-18**

8. A more lyric style of *legato* phrasing has slurs over or under note groupings. Bow direction remains intact for the duration of each slur. The amount of bow used will be determined somewhat by the tempo and dynamic level, as previously explained.

Figure **I-19**

9. Successive, repeated notes of the same pitch occurring in one-bow slurs break the normal flow of a true *legato* and require bowing adjustments. This technical discrepancy appears rather frequently in piano music where the composer seeks an over-all *legato* effect. In performance, the non-*legato* character of repeated-note attacks is minimized by applying the *portato* technique. Two alternative bowings are available to cope with this technicality. The more obvious of the two calls for a change of bow direction for the repeated note. A second and better choice in most cases is a *portato* type of bowing which does not change the direction of the bow. Instead, it merely calls for a slight stopping or lifting of the bow for note repetitions of identical pitch.

Example I-3a

Example I-3b

10. **Points for Observation.** (*a*) Successive repeated notes of the same pitch momentarily stop the movement of the bow and may change its direction. (*b*) A continuous *legato* should be confined to notes playable on a single string or on adjacent strings. (*c*) The number of notes in each slur is generally determined by the tempo and dynamic level. (*d*) *Fortissimo* passages obviously require more bow than those in the softer dynamic levels. Similarly, soft, fast *legatos* need less bow than those in the loud, slow category.

SPECIAL BOWINGS

1. *Group Staccato.* Examples I-4a and I-4b illustrate one of the several types of semi-*legato* bowings known as group *staccato*. It is a form of *portato* indicated by slurs, with dots or dashes (...)(- - -), as is found in music for all mediums. Dots, used with slurs, indicate lighter bow strokes than those necessary for the dash-slur combination (*Louré*). Both bowings tend to group into clusters the notes so marked, in a semide-tached style, especially in the faster tempos.

Example I-4a

Example I-4b

Note. The sign (·/.) indicates that the previous measure is to be repeated in total and exactly as written.

Group *staccato* bowings, when applied to repeated notes, intervals, or chords are especially useful in controlling the volume of string accompaniments to melodic lines. When so used, four to six notes in one bow is a safe maximum for the softer dynamics in moderate tempos. Three notes in one bow should not be exceeded in the *forte-fortissimo* levels.

Example I-5

(a) The bowing is that of the composer. It would be played ♩♫

Note. Passages similar to the above are occasionally bowed with the slur-dash combination for chordal progressions which benefit by extra stress and distinct separation. Dashes and dots, combined with slurs, is standard group *staccato* bowing for most long-short notations associated with the ♪♩ note cliché of the Baroque and early Classic composers. In fast tempos bow directions are reversed (♩♪).

String players have a tendency to "push" up-bows, thereby giving a false pulse and accent. This happens most frequently when a short, quick bow is followed by a longer, slow bow. Distortions of this kind can generally be remedied by using some form of group *staccato* bowing.

Example I-6

2. *Louré* is a specialized adaptation of the slur-dash type of bowing which is generally reserved for melodic phrases or for chord progressions of expressive intensity. It differs in notation from the other styles previously discussed in so far as each note within the slur is marked with a dash. *Louré* bowing is not practical in the faster tempos; its greatest effectiveness is in the medium-to-slow tempos at rather strong dynamic levels. Its true character is lost when subdued below *piano*.

Example I-7a

Example I-7b

3. *Détaché* is a non-*legato* bowing used for melodic ideas and figurations that are vigorously articulate. The bow remains on the string and the notation may or may not include dots. Although playable at most tempos, its great emphasis is felt in the medium-fast speeds with relatively few notes.

Example I-8

4. *Spiccato* bowing, frequently referred to as an "off-the-string" *staccato,* is limited to passages within a medium loud-to-soft dynamic range. Since the bow is "thrown" at the strings, the resulting tone is light and devoid of any expressive potentials. It is a bowing style demanding considerable control and is therefore somewhat hazardous, except for experienced players. Marking parts with the abbreviation *spicc.* will avoid confusion with other *staccato* bowings.

Example I-9

Joseph Wagner
Symphony No. 2

5. *Martelé* (*Martellato*) is a "hammer-stroke" style of bowing possible within a wide range of dynamics. The bow, remaining on the string, produces a dry, brittle *staccato* indicated by either dots, points, or accents. When used with the softer dynamics, the bow remains near the tip, indicated by *a punta d'arco* or *sul punta del arco*. *Forte* or *fortissimo* has the bow near the frog with the words, *du talon*.

Example I-10a

Prokofiev
Classical Symphony, Op. 25

Copyright 1926 by Edition Russe de Musique. Copyright assigned to Boosey and Hawkes 1947. By permission of the copyright owners.

Example I-10b

R. Vaughan Williams
Symphony in F minor

Example I-10c

Smetana
Overture, The Bartered Bride

6. *Jeté, saltando,* or *saltato* employs a "bouncing-bow" technique to give a semi-*staccato* bowing style restricted to the softer dynamics, *piano* and *pianissimo.* Notes are clustered in groups from three to six and are bracketed with a slur and dots usually with the word, *saltando.* This form of staccato is ideally suited to moderately fast accompaniments for wood-wind melodies (Tchaikovsky's Symphony No. 6). In fast tempos, fewer notes can be combined, as shown below.

Example I-11a

Example I-11b

7. A succession of all down-bows is a means of emphasis for occasional short progressions of chords or thematic ideas. Since the bow is lifted at the heel for each stroke, this bowing is practical only in moderate tempos. It is the strings' most powerful bowing attack.

Example I-12a

By permission of Southern Music Publishing Company, Inc., New York.

Additional examples of this bowing style are to be found in the Borodin Symphony No. 2 and the symphony *On a Mountain Air* by D'Indy.

8. The use of successive up-bows carried over several measures is a virtuoso style of bowing and occurs rarely in orchestral music. The illustration given in Example I-12b is the exception rather than the rule.

Example I-12b

9. There are two types of string tremolos—measured and unmeasured, along with two styles—bowed and fingered. Both types have rapid repetitions of notes or intervals. As for styles, the bowed-tremolo repetitions are made by the rapid movement of the bow on the string or strings. With the fingered tremolo, repetitions are made by alternating finger positions on the fingerboard while the bow moves slowly across a *single* string (as with a trill).

A measured bowed tremolo is really not a true tremolo, but an abbreviation of exact note repetitions. **Note:** *Tempo* is always the important factor in all tremolo notations.

Example I-13

Example I-13 calls for sixteen alternating down- and up-bows, illustrating the metrical correctness of a measured tremolo. This type and style of bowing has been a proven asset to composers of all periods for the reinforcement of melodic and harmonic ideas.

Example I-14a

Example I-14b

10. The bowed unmeasured tremolo differs from the measured trem-olo in so far as the repetitions are *not* metrically accurate. Confusion between the two types may be avoided for the performer by the use of proper notation and the abbreviation *trem*. In the medium-to-fast tem-pos three flags are satisfactory, with four flags being safer for all slower tempos. All shades of dynamics are possible in both types and styles of tremolos and at all speeds. This type of bowing, greatly overworked during the late 1900s, continues generally to be unused except for programmatic music, ballet, and opera scores. It does have a certain validity in passages of short duration which express agitation or the opposite extreme of restraint, since its dynamic range is enormous. Twentieth-century examples worthy of serious study can be found in the Sibelius Symphony No. 7 and in the Shostakovitch Symphony No. 5.

Example I-15a

Example I-15b

An unmeasured fingered tremolo should be confined to intervals not exceeding a diminished fifth—ones that can be played accurately on one string. The notation for the tremolo requires both notes of the interval to be properly represented according to their metrical division in each measure, the slur lengths indicating the amount of bow to be used. This style of tremolo is decidedly less agitated and powerful than its counterpart ... and is most effective for *sotto-voce*[1] effects. It was a frequent device with the Liszt-Wagner School of Romantics but has been spar-

[1] In an undertone, smothered.

ingly used since the turn of the century. At best, all forms of tremolos are limited in scope and should, therefore, be employed only when there is a valid musical justification for their effect.

Example I-16

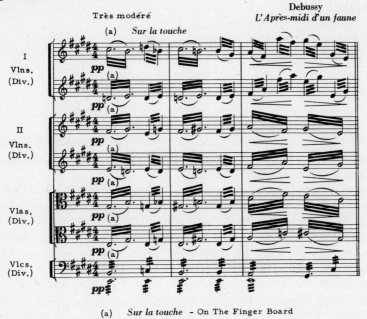

(a)   *Sur la touche* - On The Finger Board

Reprint by permission of Jean Jobert, Paris, Copyright owner, Elkan-Vogel Co., Inc., Philadelphia, Pa., agents.

Chapter 8

SPECIAL EFFECTS

Coloristic Devices
Harmonics
Double Stops and Chords

1. *Pizzicato* is the word used to indicate plucking or picking the strings with the finger tips. The abbreviation *pizz.* is sufficient, and the word *arco* written when bowing is to be resumed. The change from *arco* to *pizz.* may be made almost instantaneously if the last note preceding the *pizz.* is played with an *up*-bow. Otherwise, a few seconds of rest should be allowed for this change. Intervals, as well as three- and four-note chords, may be played *pizzicato,* an open string being a decided convenience in such combinations. Although all dynamic levels are playable—from strong, accented chords to single notes of extreme delicacy—fast tempos with rapid figurations are to be avoided as being unplayable. Soft *staccato* accompaniments, common in piano music, may frequently be transcribed effectively as string *pizzicatos.* It is imperative that the starting points for both *pizzicato* and *arco* be indicated clearly if confusion with notation is to be avoided.

Example I-17

Tchaikovsky
Symphony No. 4, Op. 36

46

Pizzicato is effective in outlining melodic figurations and rhythmical patterns. An outlining notation may be arranged by eliminating all the non-harmonic notes in a phrase or pattern.

Example I-18a   Outlining a Melodic Line

Reprinted by permission of Edward B. Marks Music Corp., New York; copyright 1944 by Edward B. Marks Corp.

Example I-18b   Outlining a Figuration

By permission of C. C. Birchard and Company, Boston.

The following suggestions should not be overlooked in writing *pizzicato* for the string section. (1) Soft octave passages in the bass are frequently arranged for *arco* cello and *pizz.* bass. (2) Avoid excessively high *pizzicato* notes. (3) Retain basic outlines eliminating rapid passage work. (4) The *pizzicato's* effectiveness is dependent upon the element of *contrast.* (5) Quick *arco-pizz.-arco* changes are possible if confined to moderately fast tempos, as illustrated in Examples I-19a and b.

Example I-19a

Example I-19b

2. The mute (*sordino* or *Dämpfer*) is a small three-pronged clamp of wood or metal which, when placed over the strings on the bridge, produces a smooth, subdued tone not possible by any other means. Mutes not only soften the tone; they change the *quality* of the tone. Muted strings create a *sotto-voce* effect that is highly desirable for quiet accompaniments with imaginative connotations. Both styles of tremolos can also be enhanced by muted string tone when confined to the softest dynamic levels. A few measures of rest are needed for the placing of mutes (termed *con sord.*), or their removal (termed *senza sord.*). An unusual organ-like effect can be produced with solo muted strings playing *pianissimo* and without *vibrato.*[1]

[1] *Vibrato* is an "artificial trembling of a note" used to vitalize tone. Orchestral strings, without *vibrato,* somewhat resemble organ tone without the tremolant stop.

Example I-20

By permission of Southern Music Publishing Co., Inc., New York.

3. *Sul ponticello* is a directive for the bow to be placed very close to the bridge. It is a bowing style which produces a "glassy," rather unmusical sound that all but obliterates pitch. Being an artificial effect, its use is restricted to music that is in the realm of the fantastic, grotesque, and mysterious. Although possible with regular detached bowing, it becomes alive when used with an unmeasured bowed tremolo. The word *naturale* (or natural) is written in the part for the resumption of normal bowing.

Example I-21

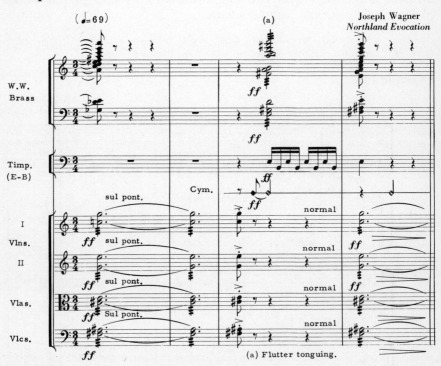

By permission of Southern Music Publishing Company, Inc., New York.

4. *Col legno* has the back of the bow striking the string, resulting in a clicking sound of rather indefinite pitch. Although composers of program music have associated this unusual bowing with the macabre, it does have interesting possibilities for abstract rhythmical ideas. The word *naturale* is used for the return to normal bowing. The eerie effect of *col legno* is fully realized in the "Witches' Sabbath" movement of the Berlioz *Symphonie fantastique*.

5. The subject of harmonics is one which merits considerable research because of its peculiarities of technique and notation. Although natural and artificial harmonics vary but slightly in sound, the methods used in playing them are quite dissimilar.

Natural harmonics (also called "*flageolet* notes") have a thin, flutey quality which is a coloristic device with an impressionistic effect. They appear infrequently as part of melodic lines and arpeggiated chords. Their greatest asset is the long, sustained inverted pedal point, sometimes augmented to include intervals and chords. Natural harmonics are produced by touching the string, without pressure, at varying points of its total length. A small circle over the note's actual pitch is the sign used.

Figure I-20 gives the natural harmonics for each open string of the violin and viola. Those for the cello would be an octave lower than those listed for the viola.

Figure I-20

Example I-22

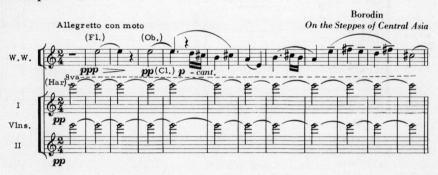

Artificial harmonics are produced by pressure applied to the first finger while the fourth finger lightly touches the string a perfect fourth above. The pitch of the note thus produced will sound two octaves above the stopped note. Artificial harmonics are indicated by placing a diamond-shaped note a perfect fourth above the stopped note. The illustrations for both types of harmonics have been left in context, since they have little or no significance by themselves.

Example I-23

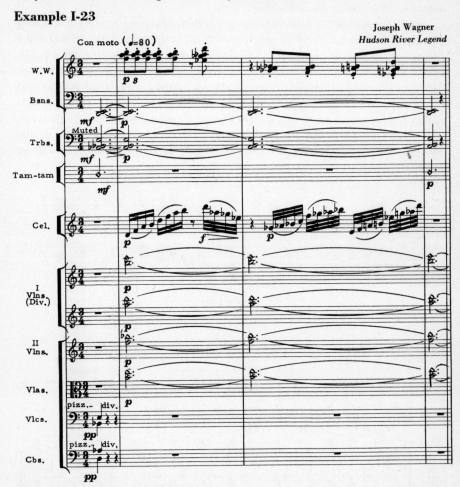

Joseph Wagner
Hudson River Legend

Harmonics, because of their uncommon timbre and pitch, are a coloristic phase of string technique rather far removed from normal, practical scoring. Conspicuously absent until the late Romantic and Impressionist periods, they have become increasingly frequent in the scores of twentieth-century composers. Representative illustrations in many and varied forms may be found in the works of Bartók, Debussy, Milhaud, Prokofiev, Ravel, and Stravinsky.

6. Double stops and chords are a natural phase of the playing tech-

nique for string instruments, but they are practical only when the intervals are confined to adjacent strings. Double stops of seconds, thirds, fourths, fifths, sixths, and octaves for violins and violas, and fifths, sixths, and octaves for cellos are playable as they "lie in the hand." The only restrictions of size for intervals having an open string as the lowest note are those concerning the player's technical proficiency in executing the full range of fingered positions. Chords of three or four notes are extensions of practical interval combinations. Keys which contain the greatest number of open-string possibilities are preferable for double stopping and chord playing. The technical skill of unprofessional string players varies greatly in this regard and it is far safer, therefore, to divide intervals and chords rather than run the risk of poor intonation or insecure attacks. The intervals and chords in Figs. I-21a and I-21b combine an open string or strings with first positions for violins, violas, and cellos. (Double stops are not practical for basses.)

Figure I-21a

Figure I-21b

Double stopping is a particular function of the second violins and violas, since most of their parts are centered in the middle-range register where extra harmony spreading is quite common. These two instruments combine very well for afterbeats in dance forms where three- and four-note chords may be set as interlocking double stops.

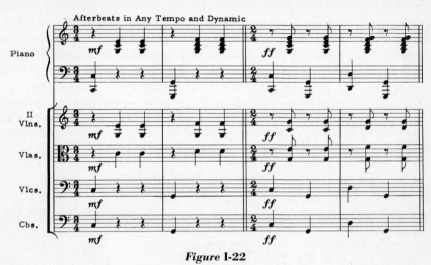

Figure I-22

Caution. Double stops are inadvisable when the top note of the intervals forms a *cantabile* melodic line. Write the two parts out *divisi*. If a two- or three-voice harmony progression is to be played *legato,* do not write double stops. Divide the parts so that a *legato* will be playable. Accurate notation for all intervals and chords is essential since it is only possible to *sustain* the two top notes.

Example I-24a

Figure I-23

Many adaptations of double stopping may be found in a variety of dynamic levels. In the softer nuances they are rarely given a *legato* bowing, while the *pizzicato* style is quite frequent. String intervals or chords may be rolled or arpeggiated, as in piano music. Perhaps their greatest worth comes from playing with successive down-bows while doubling wind instruments.

Example I-24b

By permission of J. and W. Chester Ltd., London.

7. The *glissando* (meaning "slurred, smooth, in a sliding manner") produces a smeared, unclear sound and is indicated by a straight or wavy line placed between two notes of different pitch. Sometimes the abbreviation *gliss.* or *port.* (*portamento,* meaning "to carry over") is also included. This effect, used infrequently prior to the early 1900's, has become increasingly conspicuous for all sections—strings, winds, and percussion. (See Bartók's *Concerto for Orchestra* and Morton Gould's *Latin-American Symphonette.*)

8. *Sur la touche* (or *sul tasto*), meaning "on the fingerboard," directs the bow to be placed over the fingerboard rather than in its usual place between the fingerboard and the bridge. The resulting tone becomes softer and more delicate. It is to be found mostly in scores by French composers (see Example I-16).

Chapter 9

SCORING FOR THE STRINGS

Scoring for strings, as an independent section, includes a disposition of structural developments and extensions in addition to the idiomatic arrangements of the instruments. The place of resonance in piano music has been examined and established

Structural Developments and
  Extensions
Tonal Spreads
Resonance Considerations
Doublings and Fillers
Summarized Conclusions

along with the normal distributions for four-part vocal writing. However, string settings of vocal chorals introduce new problems of spacings for instrumental resonance not heretofore considered. They also place each string instrument in its customary playing range with an emphasis on horizontal voice leading. Resonance factors, based on chordal spacings and extensions, will account for inevitable structural changes connected with the interchange of the vocal and instrumental mediums.

Example I-25

56

This setting of *America* does nothing more than double the voice parts in *unison*. The primary purpose in working with four-part choral music is to determine the ways and means by which its voice structure may be expanded in order to secure greater instrumental resonance, balance, and tonal strength. The lessons learned from these exercises can be applied to sectional or full orchestra scoring, since the basic resonance factors remain unchanged.

The first phase of converting choral parts idiomatically for strings is obtained by adding the basses *in octaves* with the cellos. A solid bass part is essential for accompaniments which may be used with large choruses. The *tessitura* of the first violin melody part, as it stands, has a minimum of vibrancy and tonal strength and would be lost if pitted against a large soprano section. If raised *an octave,* the melody, played on the E string, would sing out loud and clear. This inversion leaves the second violins and violas in hopeless positions, harmonically. These parts can be better spaced by *inverting* the alto and tenor voices. **Note:** Spacing inadequacies in the middle register can generally be satisfactorily revised by inverting the alto and tenor voices whenever the ranges of the melody and/or bass parts are changed. These suggestions have been applied to the scoring in Example I-26.

Example I-26

The same need for good voice leading applies to orchestral parts as to the writing of four-part harmonizations. Consecutive fifths or octaves resulting from added fillers or doublings are not considered objectionable since they are inevitable in most expanded triad progressions in the treble clef.

The following four settings of *America* vary structurally from six to ten voice parts. Examples I-27a and I-27b differ in the arrangement of the three inside parts.

Example I-27a

Example I-27b

The eight parts in Example I-27c represent the maximum sonority possible in this voice distribution without any new changes in the ranges of the melody or the bass.

Example I-27c

Comparison of this eight-part setting with Example I-25 reveals all four original voices doubled in the octave. A seven-part version is possible by removing the inverted alto voice.

Example I-27d

Ten Parts

This ten-part plan is possible only when five-string basses are available. In this connection, it is of importance to note the *tessitura* problems caused by key tonalities. Any key a major third higher than G would assure greater brilliance and sonority—first, by the raised pitch, and secondly, by providing better tonal spreads for normal instrumental ranges. The four inside voices of this arrangement, in the bass part, have special interest because they do not follow rigid chord progressions. Rather, these progressions were selected for the following reasons: (1) to prevent fundamental triad positions; (2) to retain common tones whenever possible; and (3) to avoid unnecessary consecutive fifths and octaves.

This arrangement could be further extended for three additional voices in the treble, but the *tessitura* of the top notes would then be playable only by the piccolo.

Picc.
Fls.

Figure I-24

8va.

Picc.
Fls.

Figure I-25

In general, fillers should not be added *above* the melodic line as they tend to obscure its clarity. This point does not refer to added counterpoints, figurations, or arabesques which do not affect the tonal profile of the leading part. High-octave melody doublings without fillers are possible and sometimes desirable if adequately supported by well-spaced middle-range and bass parts.

The conclusions to be drawn from working with four-part choral music for orchestra are:

1. Limited range means limited resonance and tonal strength.

2. All voice parts are independent units with horizontal freedom and movement.

3. Thick part writing in the bass register is to be avoided.

4. All models discussed thus far are suitable for sectional or full-orchestra scoring.

5. Before adding fillers, experiment with inverted alto and tenor parts.

6. Overpadding with doublings and fillers leads to unbalanced sonorities.

7. Melodies should not be inserted arbitrarily between harmony parts.

Note. The author's use of *America* as a model for settings of four-part music (chorals) in his book, *Band Scoring, A Comprehensive Manual,* will enable students to make definitive examinations and comparisons of this phase of scoring for both the orchestra and band media.

Chapter 10

REFERENCE CHART OF KEYBOARD IDIOMS AND PATTERNS

The previous subject matter, dealing with the strings, gave an insight into the fundamental assets and liabilities of the section as a whole. Ways and means of tone production, development of harmonic textures and resonance

> *Standardization of Transcription Media as a Basic Formula for the Reference Chart as Applied to the String Section*

values and factors have been analyzed, evaluated, and classified. These prerequisites are valuable in acting as a background to the actual study of idiomatic string writing as it applies to the formulas and textures of music for keyboard instruments. Even a casual survey of music in these categories reveals certain technical formulas that appear rather consistently and as integral parts of compositional techniques. Closer examination shows that these technical matters can, in many instances, be isolated from their context and classified as concrete examples of keyboard idioms and patterns.

The *Reference Chart* has been designed to analyze these technicalities and to readapt them to orchestral dimensions. Thus, each entry in the *Chart* becomes a specific technical problem which, when properly disposed of, serves as a model for all subsequent repetitions of the same or similar technicalities.

Since the string section is the very backbone of the orchestra, it is advisable to apply all of the subject matter of the *Reference Chart* to it, as an independent unit. By so doing, each entry can be examined, analyzed, and applied, thus providing the basis for the subsequent addition of wind and percussion instruments. It is of the utmost importance for the orchestrator to acquire some facility with this transcribing process since practical orchestration is dependent upon the dispositions made of the string section. Good scoring habits thus initiated become an integral part of a good scoring technique.

61

REFERENCE CHART OF
KEYBOARD IDIOMS AND PATTERNS

I. BROKEN INTERVALS
1. Broken octaves
2. Broken octaves with embellishments
3. Broken octaves combined with thirds
4. Broken sixths
5. Broken thirds
6. Broken sixths and thirds combined

II. BROKEN CHORDS
1. Left-hand broken chords in close position
2. Left-hand broken chords in open position
3. Broken chords spaced for two hands
4. Broken chords in right hand with implied melodic line
5. Broken chords with blocked melodic and rhythmic patterns
6. Arpeggiated chords

III. MELODIC LINES AND FIGURATIONS
1. Large melodic skips
2. Outlining a melodic line
3. Dividing a melodic line
4. Melodic lines combined with repeated note patterns; nonmetrical passages
5. Melodic settings: contrasts, comparative strengths, and repeated phrases

IV. IMPLIED BASS PARTS

V. SINGLE-NOTE, INTERVAL, AND CHORD REPETITIONS

VI. TWO- AND THREE-PART MUSIC
1. Homophonic
2. Polyphonic
3. Style mixtures

VII. SPACING PROBLEMS IN THE MIDDLE REGISTER
1. Large harmonic gaps
2. Sustained notes, intervals, and chords

VIII. CONTRAST PROBLEMS CONDITIONED BY DYNAMICS

IX. VOICE LEADING

X. OBBLIGATO OR ADDED SECONDARY PARTS ARRANGED FROM HARMONIC PROGRESSIONS

XI. ANTIPHONAL EFFECTS

XII. TREMOLO TYPES

XIII. DANCE FORMS (Afterbeats)

I. BROKEN INTERVALS

Repeated intervals and chords are generally avoided in piano music, being unidiomatic and unpianistic. The composer of piano music approximates the *effect* of repetition by means of broken or arpeggiated intervals or chords. It is a technical expedient playable at most dynamic levels and tempos. However, as repetitions of notes and intervals present no difficulties for the string player, most *broken intervals* can be efficiently transcribed as *repeated intervals* without losing their identity.

1. Broken Octaves

a. Bass register

Example S-1

Example S-1 *(continued)*

The broken octaves in this example have been arranged to offer some contrast between the starting *piano* and the following *crescendo* measures and may serve as a model for all subsequent intervals in this category. The bass part at (2) emphasizes the pulse of the repeated C's in the cello part while the added quarter notes, starting in the fifth measure, give greater strength and vitality to the *crescendo* of the last measures. The omission of the viola part (1) points up the fact that instruments should not be used "just to fill in." Actually, this delayed entrance of the violas creates a new interest.

Attention should be given to the rearrangement of the directional lines of the second violin and viola parts at (3). This change compensates for the rising melodic line in the first violin part and the necessity of having the progression in open position (4). Close positions can be resumed as the bass part rises in contrary motion to the melodic line, with the intervals to be played as double stops (non-*divisi*).

b. Treble register

Example S-2

The moderately slow tempo and soft dynamic here makes three versions of this broken octave possible—a literal transcription in addition to the two ways given here. In the faster tempos with stronger dynamics, the version with the repeated octave is advised.

Attention is also directed here to the scoring of the duet phrase in the lower treble since it places the violas *above* the second violins. This has been done in order to take advantage of the viola's unique tonal color in this register as compared to the violin. It is an application of the fact made earlier that the high and low strings are more distinctive than the middle ones.

2. Broken Octaves with Embellishments

Example S-3

For practical purposes this Beethoven excerpt can be divided into two parts: the rising scale coupled with the embellished A in the bass and the broken embellished octaves in the treble starting in the fifth measure. The repetition of melody with its changed *tessitura* is another salient feature. The embellished A (1) has been raised an octave so that the two-octave gap in the middle register will be eliminated and a better balance achieved between the octave melody and the rising bass part. With the dynamic of *piano,* the *pizz.* bass will give ample support to the *arco* cellos.

At (2) the grace note indicates the need of a sustained octave for the last four measures. The broken embellished octaves, starting at (3) in the divided violin parts, establish a pattern for this figuration. The second violin part here maintains the broken-octave effect. However, if stronger dynamics are used, it would be advisable to repeat the figure literally in the lower octave. At (4) the last three notes of the viola part have been raised an octave as the low B is not playable and the original *tessitura* of these three notes, if not changed, would cause an undesirable spacing problem in the middle register.

3. Broken Octaves Combined with Thirds

Example S-4

The setting of this excerpt at [a] is adequate at all speeds and dynamics but will obviously be non-*legato*. A *legato* effect in fast tempos is possible with all broken intervals with one part played as repeated notes provided the other part[1] is played *legato* [b]. For moderate-to-slow tempos, the settings given at [c] and [d] may be used with discretion for the medium-to-soft dynamics.

4. Broken Sixths

There are two major considerations involved in transcribing a series of *legato* broken sixths as here indicated by Beethoven. The continuous eighth-note movement must be maintained—*legato*—throughout the passage. The problem is to integrate these characteristics so that they will be idiomatically practicable.

Example S-5

_____

[1] The highest part whenever possible.

Example S-5 *(continued)*

This adaptation of broken sixths applies the principle of having one *legato* part combined with a second, non-*legato* part carrying out the rhythmic notation. It is a setting possible at all tempos and dynamic levels.

At (1) the first violins are divided in octaves to compensate for the stronger *forte* dynamic as well as to fill the need for greater sonority as the figure ascends to a higher range. The entrance of the bass part at (2) requires a three-octave spread to avoid the large gap in the middle register and to add emphasis value to this part.

5. Broken Thirds

There is very little difference between the method of arranging these intervals for strings and that given for sixths. The type of adaptation will be determined by the style, tempo, and dynamic of the passage in question.

Similar treatment can, of course, be applied to broken intervals in the tenor and/or bass ranges as shown in Examples S-6c and d. The versions given at Examples S-6a and c are called for in fast tempos while those at Examples S-6b and d are playable in most moderate and slow tempos. (See the second movement of Beethoven's Sixth Symphony for string parts in broken thirds.) The upper eighth-note stems (cello) in Example S-6c have an alternative modification which permits a *legato* effect for broken intervals at fast tempos.

Example S-6

Continuous *legato* thirds are possible only when arranged as indicated at (1). This contrary-motion principle, if applied to repeated chords (Fig. S-1b), will allow the full chord to sound with *legato* phrasing.

Figure S-1a

Figure S-1b

6. Broken Sixths and Thirds Combined

Transcription of intervals in this category follows the same principles given for Examples S-4 and S-5. String transcriptions of all broken intervals should include complete interval representation along with basic rhythmic notation.

Example S-7

II. BROKEN CHORDS

1. Left-hand Broken Chords in Close Position

Example S-8

The second-violin part, derived from the harmony (1), fills the harmonic gap created by the rising melodic line. One moving part in eighth notes (viola) is sufficient here for the *piano* dynamic. The repeated F's in the cello supply the rhythmic pulse for each measure (2). This excerpt is an example of homophonic two-part writing expanded idiomatically for four voices. It has the texture of string quartet music.

Example S-9

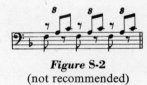

Figure S-2
(not recommended)

This excerpt continues the study of close-position chords but with a different rhythmic pattern and a changed melodic problem in the treble. The octave melody is continued in the first violins at (1). Fifths of triads serve well as starting and sustaining notes for common tones in chord progressions (second violins). The triplet figure in the viola part (3) derives from the top notes of the original piano triplet. Rearranged figurations of this kind should consist of the smallest possible intervals, always moving toward the nearest positions of succeeding chord tones. The cello bowing at (2) is recommended for extracted bass parts with similar notation. The bass *pizz.* (4) defines the rhythmic pulse of each measure. Triplet notations, as used here, should not be transcribed as in Fig. S-2 except in slow tempos.

Example S-10

Mozart
Sonata No. 3

Broken close-position chords in low ranges present entirely new difficulties not associated with those in the middle register. Chords in this category will need redistribution retaining the rhythmic element and *tessitura* of the lowest bass notes. These changes can be examined by comparing the parts (3, 4, 5) with the original chord positions. Added harmonic fillers (1) are worthy of part interest whenever possible. Their design and movement will be influenced by the context of the passage. (*Musical context,* as used here, includes all pertinent elements of style, texture, phrasing, and dynamics which can influence a presentation.) Intentional octave passages (6) should remain free of harmonizations.

2. Left-hand Broken Chords in Open Position

Example S-11

The use of the damper pedal is significant in planning the scoring of this excerpt, for it indicates the need of a maximum string sonority. The descending chromatic line (2) with the continued E combines with the divided cellos (3) to complete the chord structure, the *pizz.* bass (4) giving the rhythmic pulsation which can be sustained slightly by means of *vibrato.* Transcription of the treble parts is literal (1). Enharmonics (viola part—fourth measure) are often a desirable device for promoting better intonation with most string players, especially when C♭ and F♭ are involved.

Example S-12

Another setting of chords in this classification (Example S-12) is given to show the addition of a second rhythmic part (1) which includes the outlining bass notes so essential to the stability of the harmonic progressions. The ranges and tonal strength of the melodic treble justify this addition.

Example S-13

Further application of the principles used in the two previous examples may be applied to this progression by Brahms. This figuration, broken into two parts, has the thirds continuously in the violas, while the cellos and bass combine to clarify the bass part. **Note:** The D at (1) is possible only on a five-string bass.

3. Broken Chords Spaced for Two Hands

Example S-14

The broken chords in this example have two distinct points of interest. First, there is the necessity of establishing the continuous sixteenth-note motion for the first three measures. The second concerns the two contrasting melodic lines which can be extracted from the first and last notes (lows and highs) of the progression.

The given *forte* dynamic suggests *tutti* scoring with a maximum of sonority. The implied melodic lines in the treble and bass are spaced so that the double rhythmic parts in the second violins and violas can function freely. This scoring plan has cohesion within a prescribed range spread.

Although this example is concerned chiefly with broken chords spaced for two hands, it is also a good illustration of quasi-contrapuntal entrances (1) as well as of troublesome distributions of melodic and harmonic elements as found in the piano original (2). The entrances at (1) have been arranged to give an antiphonal effect, with the violin parts of the last four measures covering the range of the full melodic line (2). The close-position chords in the bass (3) have been opened to supply harmonic balance for the revised treble parts. In general, it should be established that numerous broken-chord progressions in this classification will not always be adaptable to string transcription, for pianistic music, at its best, is least practicable when transcribed for orchestra.

Example S-15a

This two-part succession of broken chords for two hands is included in this discussion in an effort to show various ways of adaptation not casually obvious. It presents a challenge to the idea of "making something out of nothing" in a structural sense. These two parts in contrary motion clearly indicate an implied melodic line and harmonic progression. It may therefore be rearranged from either of these points of view depending upon its place in a full context.

Example S-15b

Ibid.

Example S-15c

Ibid.

The rhythmic second-violin part in Example S-15b acts as a central pivot for the literal first violin and viola parts. The inclusion of the cello is for further sustained unity, and its use would be optional, depending upon the full context of the passage. In Example S-15c, the two outside parts outline the implied melodic design while the inside parts remain unchanged from the original version.

Example S-15d

Example S-15e

When this type of transcription is desired, the two parts may be assigned to any instruments capable of playing them in their entirety and without unnecessary range difficulties. There is a unique example of this style of two-part writing in the middle of the *Adagio* section of Saint-Saëns' Symphony No. 3. Here, the composer establishes a dialogue of two-part counterpoint similar to the Mozart excerpt previously discussed, which subsequently serves as a background on which the principal melodic material is superimposed.

These illustrations effectively demonstrate the premise that there may be several ways of orchestrating a given phrase or passage, each quite different from the other, but each quite possibly correct. The final choice must, as always, be governed by the appropriateness of the scoring within a specific musical context.

4. Broken Chords in Right Hand with Implied Melodic Line

Example S-16

Example S-16 *(continued)*

A string adaptation of this typical example of Mozartian pianistic music entails considerable readjustment to insure adequate representation of its salient features. Careful examination of the triplet figuration will reveal an independent melodic line which must be integrated with the isolated two-note phrases occurring in the measures with the cross-hand parts. Other notes within the triplet movement are good material for secondary parts in the treble. The real problem lies in maintaining idiomatically a *legato* effect for the middle strings without resorting to out-of-proportion technical difficulties. The version given here seeks to arrive at the general *legato* effect through the use of one or two sustained parts paired with repeated notes.

5. Broken Chords with Blocked Melodic and Rhythmic Patterns

Example S-17

Example S-17 *(continued)*

The setting of this vigorous Beethoven passage follows the basic method used for Example S-16, though not neglecting differences of dynamics and ranges. Its spacing and style are affected by the *stretto*,[1] the embellished D pedal point and the general *legato* phrasing in the first eight measures.

It is desirable, when possible, to reduce music in this category to four-part structure. By so doing, all voice lines fall into natural ranges which otherwise might seem obscure. In this example, the application of this method automatically necessitates raising the embellished pedal point an octave (1) so as to facilitate full chord representation. The bass part (2), with its unison *pizz.-arco,* emphasizes the cello as being the true bass instrument of the string section, not the contrabasses, as might be imagined. **Note:** In general, it is advisable not to write single-line bass parts for the contrabasses without unison or doubling of some kind. The bowing for all the strings here has been arranged to produce an accumulative effect of sonority and tension as indicated by the *stretto.*

Other species of broken chords are best transcribed by means of the measured bowed tremolo. It requires a notation which will retain the same rhythmical values but with reduced chord spreads. It is playable at all tempos and dynamic levels.

[1] Overlapping or piling up of short bits of thematic material.

Example S-18

Although this example is primarily concerned with the disposition of broken chords, it also covers spacing for the close-position chords in the bass part. The *fortissimo* dynamic requires a maximum of sonority which, in this case, can be aided by double stopping for the violas and cellos.

6. Arpeggiated Chords

String arrangement of arpeggiated chords differ from their pianistic counterparts in one important respect; it is a technicality to which the non-string player must pay particular attention. Piano chords in this category usually have the repetitions of full chord spreads arranged so that no notes are repeated successively, either within the chord limits or in its repetitions. Pianistic technique allows interval skips up to an octave, downward or upward, for repetitions but not repeated notes of the same pitch.

However, string-arpeggiated chords are idiomatic only when repeated notes of the *same pitch* occur as starting notes for each change of bow. This is a technical expedient which cannot be ignored or overlooked.

Example S-19

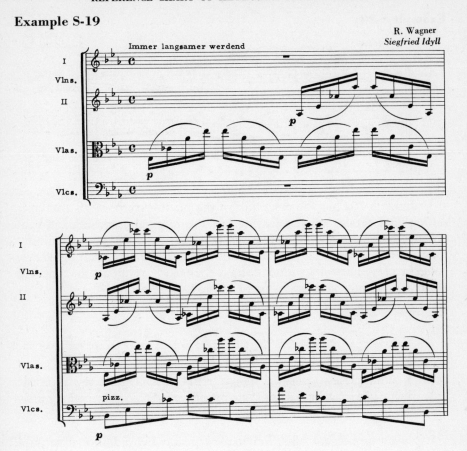

III. MELODIC LINES AND FIGURATIONS

1. Large Melodic Skips

Large melodic skips in all forms and sizes are natural characteristics of music for keyboard instruments where no intonation difficulties exist. Unfortunately, string players must "make their own pitch," which automatically raises the spectre of possible faulty intonation, especially for rapid passages with non-diatonic large intervals. Passages containing questionable interval patterns in this category may frequently be revised idiomatically for strings by dividing them into two parts arranged to relieve awkward skips, yet retaining the full flavor of the original.

Example S-20a

Example S-20a has the essentials of the piano excerpt in an advisable setting that retains all the features of the original: phrasing, off-beat accents, and basic one-voice texture. It is playable at all speeds and dynamic levels. **Note:** In moderate-to-slow tempos, the original figuration could be played literally, with one slight change which utilizes the repeated note plan for bow changes as in Example S-20b.

Example S-20b

If played non-*legato,* this Weber excerpt has two additional settings which change its texture but add sonority and rhythmic drive. Both are further illustrations of the diversification possible from limited source material.

Example S-20c

Example S-20d

Example S-21 combines broken chords with broken octaves to be played *fortissimo*. This dynamic may be best achieved by dividing this figuration into two parts so that a maximum of speed and sonority can be maintained.

Example S-21

Here, the pianistic sequence is decidedly awkward for strings and requires divisions which will keep the parts within limited ranges, thereby preventing undue shifting of positions. In this connection, it is advisable to maintain rhythmic patterns once established.

Example S-22

In the final analysis, all revisions of melodic lines with large skips must be determined by the extenuating provisions of tempo and dynamic level. Certainly, it is far more preferable to have idiomatic string writing than to needlessly force string players into figurations and phrases which belong under the fingers of a pianist.

Example S-23

Although professional violinists would have no major intonation difficulties with a literal playing of this melody, players with less technical skill might experience uncertainties with intonation. For that reason, division of the melody, as given, is desirable if the treble part is to sound natural and unforced.

2. Outlining a Melodic Line

The study made of the previous classification is a good prerequisite for outlining a melodic line, since both subjects are workable by much the same technique. Most examples in this category combine a rhythmic figuration with an implied melodic line. By isolating these elements, two distinct and independent parts can be formed. These separate parts may be determined by applying the principles of harmonic analysis. Once the melody in most elemental form is established, its rhythmic counterpart can be adjusted to fit the rhythmic representation of the original.

Example S-24

Example S-25

Example S-26

Example S-27

By permission of R. D. Row Music Company, Boston.

3. Dividing a Melodic Line

Subject matter in this classification follows rather closely along the lines established for the previous two *Reference Chart* entries. The purpose here is to not only revise melodies with possible large intervals, but to intentionally develop a two-voice structure which will add interest and variety to otherwise static harmonic fillers. In Example S-28 this theory is practiced, resulting in a dialogue for the violins which retains the salient features of the original piano theme.

Example S-28

The divided melodic line for the second violin in Example S-28 eliminates the middle-gap tonal voids between the original treble and tenor parts and makes a smooth transition to the harmonic filler at (1).

4. Melodic Lines Combined With Repeated Note Patterns

Example S-29

Allegro ($\bullet$ = 126)

Beethoven
Sonata, Op. 10, No. 3

Example S-29 *(continued)*

Whenever melodic lines are combined with repeated note patterns, it will be necessary to separate these elements according to their respective functional uses. Frequent dislocations of normal spacing can be expected in this category, resulting from purely keyboard considerations. The orchestrator's task is to achieve maximum sonority from a revised structure which places each string part in its most advantageous playing position.

The first step in this process is to insure the continuous repetition of the rhythmic pattern, spaced to allow unhampered representation of each entrance as it occurs. For this reason, the viola part (1) has been raised an octave and, in this *tessitura*, will have clarity and coherence in addition to avoiding subsequent middle-register harmonic voids. Furthermore, rapid notes in very low ranges are never clear, especially when two voices are set in the same timbre, for they always result in a meaningless rumble of sound rather than articulate note pitches. A distinction of difference can be made in this connection. If one moving part (cello) is combined with one stationary part (bass) there will be less chance of "thickness" in these parts (2). The octave double stop here (3) adds tonal strength for the cadence. Study should also be directed to the first measure with its special adjustments due to the missing F♯ in the second violins.

Nonmetrical Passages. Uneven, cadenza-like groupings of notes, which cannot be metrically divided, are best transcribed for a solo instrument, as they are impractical in any other form (4).

Example S-30

The rhythmic treble part in Example S-30 is a typical pianistic device which is not literally applicable to strings, except in very slow tempos and dance forms which have note pulsation with afterbeats. The continuity of the rhythmic pattern is maintained in the second violins and violas, while the interchange of *pizz.* in the first violins and cellos brightens up the passage considerably. Note the continuance of the viola part at (1).

5. Melodic Settings: Contrasts, Comparative Strengths, and Repeated Phrases

Finding the proper setting for a melody in orchestration is a matter of prime importance. When the leading melodic line in any passage can be set off clearly from its surrounding counterparts (rhythmic figurations, sustained harmony parts, secondary counterpoints, and *obbligatos*), the way has been cleared to secure the first element of balance. A number of factors contribute to the realization of this distinguishing quality.

a. Contrast. The element of contrast is vital to all scoring if it is to be alive. A melody which remains endlessly in the same range and timbre is apt to become a dead melody.

b. Tonal Strengths. The orchestrator's task is to provide clarity of definition in all parts. This element of balance may be attained through an understanding of comparative instrumental strengths. There is considerable variety in the tonal strengths of string instruments as a result of inherent differences in their playing *ranges*. The highest strings in each instance have far greater tonal strength than the two middle strings. On the other hand, the lowest strings have a rich, sonorous quality which carries well.

c. Spacing. Every important phrase needs freedom of movement. To accomplish this, all component parts require spacings which will allow definition while recognizing the characteristic timbre of each instrument and its strong and weak playing ranges.

d. Repeated Melodic Phrases. Phrases in this category may acquire extra tonal interest through the contrast of timbres and playing *tessituras*. The orchestrator can extend this phase of scoring with short, antiphonal canonic imitations.

IV. IMPLIED BASS PARTS

All the subject matter under section III is pertinent to implied bass parts. Actually, the methods used for the extraction and arrangement of two parts from a single voice line in either the treble or bass registers remain unchanged. It is the line of direction which changes. In working with this problem in the treble range, the implied melody was always apparent from combinations of the highest notes. Extracting implied bass parts reverses this directional process, for here the lowest bass notes in a single voice line usually become the ones which can constitute an independent bass part. Voice lines adaptable to this treatment frequently appear as broken chords and at other times as mixed tenor-bass parts. When these phrases occur, the lowest notes usually have frequent repetitions thus establishing implied bass parts.

The advisability of using implied bass parts can be settled only after the following questions have been analyzed and answered: (1) What is the texture of the music? (2) In what context does the passage occur? (3) Would the addition of an implied bass part help or hinder a phrase which might be played as one voice and by one instrument? (4) Should an added bass part remain in its original *tessitura* or should it be lowered an octave to give support to the harmonic structure? (5) Will the division of a single voice line upset the balance and natural flow of the original part? These are the questions that the orchestrator must answer with musical judgment before taking action in this area, since unwise adaptations can lead to disastrous results.

Examples S-31a and S-31b are two versions of the same bass part with extracted implied melodic lines. Differences between the two settings are those of *tessituras* (violas and cellos) and range spreads (violins).

Example S-31a

Example S-31b

V. SINGLE-NOTE, INTERVAL, AND CHORD REPETITIONS

The purpose of further study of this classification is concerned solely with the variety of ways in which repeated notes in any form may occur in keyboard music and their possible adaptations for strings.

1. Repeated Notes—without Rests

Example S-32

2. Repeated Notes—with Rests

Example S-33

Mendelssohn
Song without Words, Op. 38, No. 2

3. Repeated Intervals as Afterbeats

Example S-34

Schubert
Moment Musical, Op. 94, No. 3

Occasionally, passages occur in piano music with divided repeated-note patterns alternating between the two hands. This pianistic device is variable in both structure and dynamic levels. As literal transcription is impractical, the best approach to orchestral adaptation is by reducing the full passage to its most elementary rhythmic plan. From this reduction, new idiomatic dispositions can be made of the melodic and harmonic elements, free of pianistic implications.

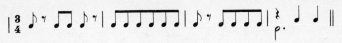

Figure S-3

Example S-35

Rebikov
Danse des dryades, Op. 14

Figure S-4

Example S-36

Figure S-5

The objective in scoring passages similar to Example S-36 must be to arrange proper representation of both the rhythmic figures and harmonic parts when they occur. Often these elements can be combined as shown at (1). Notice how the voice lines are continued at (2) and not dropped an octave as in the original at (3). The rhythmic-harmonic plan follows the outline given in Fig. S-4.

Example S-37 shows an enharmonic for the viola at (2) since the B below is not on the instrument. The repeated notes at (1) are as indicated in Fig. S-5.

Example S-37

VI. TWO- AND THREE-PART MUSIC

Music may be stylistically divided into two categories—*homophonic* and *polyphonic,* each in turn having a direct bearing on its respective texture. These textures present certain specific problems in orchestration.

They are soluble only through an evaluation of the musical intentions of the composer in the realms of compositional techniques and structural styles. The orchestrator's major concern in scoring music in this category should be governed by accepted practices covering the place of harmony in these two distinctly different styles. Two- and three-part passages are standard textures for much keyboard music. They are, however, less general in orchestral music and should therefore be examined in detail for their full implications.

1. Homophonic

Homophonic music may best be described as a single melody with a harmonic accompaniment. Neither the number of parts nor their harmonic complexity alters this definition. With it there is an absence of formalized counterpoint, although good voice leading may be present.

Music in this category may frequently benefit from the addition of harmonic fillers, especially in middle registers. However, their inclusion should not alter melodic or bass ranges. Actual notation for fillers can be determined only after the implied harmonic progressions have been analyzed. When added, they should conform to the principles of good voice leading. The following examples have been planned for analysis of this classification:

Example S-38

This excerpt is a mixture of two- and three-part writing in the homophonic style. The second violin and viola fillers follow the established rhythmic designs of the treble and bass, which is desirable in maintaining continuity. The *pizzicato* bass part gives the right support without being too heavy.

Example S-39

Here, the consistent interval of a third in the tenor range establishes a three-part homophonic texture. The repeated low D's in the bass on second beats set up a fourth voice for the cellos and basses.

Example S-40

This excerpt is one of especial interest inasmuch as its two-part structure might cause some ambiguity in the matter of style. Frequently, music of this kind can be played literally by appropriate solo strings or wood-winds. However, any attempted scoring in this form—for full strings—would result in clumsily arranged piano music. Although the part writing appears to be contrapuntal, the chord progressions are sufficiently established to permit a homophonic approach in scoring it. To accomplish this, its full harmonic implications should be converted to idiomatic voice parts developed as given under Close-position Chords (II-1) and Implied Bass Parts (IV).

Example S-41

Example S-41 illustrates embellished octaves *without* harmonization. It further shows the contrast value of changing ranges to conform to changing dynamics.

2. Polyphonic

Polyphonic music is the exact antithesis of homophonic music. It incorporates the principles of counterpoint, defined as "the art of adding one or more parts to a given part according to certain rules." However, this time-honored definition applies to *strict* counterpoint, and composers have long since abandoned this rigidity of rule. It is a compositional style with a formalized application of all the devices of counterpoint, with emphasis on part writing rather than harmonization. The number and complexity of voice parts may vary, but the texture of contrapuntal passages remains quite consistent. It is music basically conceived and executed in terms of horizontal part writing. Vertical considerations become involved primarily when harmonic problems arise from abnormal chromaticism, multiple counterpoints, and/or added harmonizations.

Orchestration of music in this style and texture needs part definition and clarity. Following are a few suggestions for carrying out details of scoring:

a. All entering parts with principal thematic material should have superior tonal strength and weight. This may be achieved through contrasts with surrounding timbres and/or by doubled unison parts for emphasis.

b. Instruments chosen for each theme should be able to carry it through in its entirety.

c. Subject and answer passages are not generally effective if scored for divided, identical timbres, except for climaxes with full orchestra.

d. Harmonizations should not be added unless included in the original.

e. Dynamics can be adjusted to accommodate the relative importance of each contrapuntal line.

Example S-42

Each entry of the subject in this *fugato* is doubled for extra tonal strength but the countersubjects revert to single parts. The down-bows and unison winds give accents where needed.

3. Style Mixtures

Composers, for more than three centuries, have made frequent juxtapositions of the homophonic and polyphonic styles. It is this very interplay of style textures which has characterized the continual growth of symphonic music as an art form. However, this musical duality did not reach its zenith until the time of Haydn and Mozart. Yet its roots are discernible in the works of many of the more distinguished names of the Baroque period.

Two widely different parts of the *Well-tempered Clavichord* by Johann Sebastian Bach demonstrate clearly the differences between these two styles. The C major Prelude is a rare forerunner of one type of homophonic music, being an extended series of broken chords. But the four-voice Fugue which follows is contrapuntal music at its formal best.

Similar analogies of symphonic music for orchestra are numerous. The Largo from Antonín Dvořák's *New World* Symphony is homophonic music with occasional secondary themes devoid of formalized contrapuntal devices. This music moves essentially by *vertical* progressions. Conversely, the third-movement coda of Paul Hindemith's symphony *Mathis der Maler* is *horizontally* conceived and executed. Here, the composer sets up an *ostinato* with secondary counterpoints on which a choral-like melody is superimposed with telling effect. It is the orchestrator's task to recognize and differentiate between these two styles of composition and to score them accordingly.

Example S-43

Beethoven
Sonata, Op. 10, No. 3

Example S-43 *(continued)*

Example S-43 is a good illustration of style mixtures and affords excellent source material for analysis. The modification of the octave skip at (1) and (2) allows the complete subject to remain in the cello part. The unison at (3) gives tonal strength to the final entrance of the subject in the middle register. The homophonic phase of this excerpt starts with the four-part chordal writing at (4). The up-bow change at (5) facilitates the *crescendo* which follows. At (6) the second-violin part continues the harmonic filler without disrupting the other parts. The lower part of the third at (7) has been inverted an octave to avoid a middle-register harmonic gap. Open positions at (8) and the spacing at (9) have been made in the interest of increased sonority for the *crescendo*. The entrance of the basses at (10) supports the sudden *sforzando* and merges smoothly with the cellos for the ensuing octaves.

VII. SPACING PROBLEMS IN THE MIDDLE REGISTER

1. Large Harmonic Gaps

The very nature of idiomatic piano writing admits numberless patterns which require the left hand to be in the bass range while the right hand is occupied with passages far removed in the middle and upper reaches of the treble. While this kind of writing may be successful for piano music, it often poses serious problems for the orchestrator. Although there may be isolated instances where large middle-harmonic gaps are justifiable, the usual procedure of avoiding them by a rearrangement of the voice parts is recommended. In this kind of adaptation, it is vital to arrive at idiomatic orchestral part writing which embodies all of the salient features of the original while disposing of the causes of unbalanced structures.

Usually such adaptations necessitate the changing of all close-position chordal elements in the bass parts to open position, along with the rearrangement of some of the secondary parts in the treble. If balance is to be achieved and maintained between these parts, it is imperative in practical orchestration that there be no unnatural large harmonic gaps in between. This subject has been discussed in a number of previous examples in conjunction with other entries of the *Reference Chart*. The following example serves to illustrate this subject matter as it pertains to structural problems.

Example S-44

The arrangement of the melody-harmony parts in the treble of the first two measures is of special interest. It represents a recommended solution for eliminating harmonic gaps and, at the same time, for creating good voice leading for the middle-harmony parts. The occasional overlapping of the viola with the second violin in these measures will not seriously interfere with this part.

2. Sustained Notes, Intervals, and Chords

Another phase of middle-register voids concerns not only the readjustment of structural elements but the place of resonance and the means for securing it. This aspect of orchestration differs in proportion to the instrumentation for each piece. Where a minimum of parts is available, as in sectional scoring, the problem is more acute. Resonance, as secured by sustained notes, intervals, and chords, should be adjudged according to the needs of each passage, for it is a variable factor.

Example S-45

The disposition of the treble part has been previously examined in Example S-25. The difficulty here concerns a string adaptation of the broken-chord cross rhythm in the bass part, which is obviously far removed from a literal approach. If the starting figuration is rearranged for the cellos as given, the basses can outline the chords while the violas provide middle-range resonance. When the violas take over the figuration at (1), the cellos can sustain the outlining chord tones. As both treble and bass parts approach closer positions with a decreased dynamic, the total range can be contracted by eliminating the basses at (2).

VIII. CONTRAST PROBLEMS CONDITIONED BY DYNAMICS

Contrast in orchestration is secured not only by differentials of timbres, tonal strengths, and weights, but also by structural variations in total ranges. This latter element is conditioned, to a large degree, by dynamics, as they serve as a guide in determining the amount and kind of sonority and resonance appropriate for each phrase and/or passage. An application of this cause-and-effect aspect of scoring is demonstrated in the two versions given for Examples S-46a and b, with their changed dynamics.

Example S-46

Chopin
Valse, Op. 34, No. 2

Comparison of these examples shows the effect of changing dynamics on range, chord spacing, texture, and balance. Maximum tonal spreads not only affect the *tessituras* of the two outside parts, but likewise necessitate redistribution of the inner voices. The effect of dynamics therefore exceeds the limitation of volume, being inseparably associated with relative tonal strengths and tonal spreads.

IX. VOICE LEADING

Good voice leading is a mark of distinction and one which generally spells the difference between the amateur and the professional. It is a developed skill which can be acquired through study, practice, and application. Its roots stem from the divergent conceptions of vertical harmonic progressions and horizontal contrapuntal part writing. The following suggestions are given as aids for facilitating good voice leading in orchestral thinking.

1. View each voice line in terms of *horizontal*—not vertical—movement.

2. Consider the forward movement of all chord tones as separate voices.

3. Evaluate, in context, the function of all harmonic fillers as independent voice parts whenever possible.

4. Apply contrapuntal devices when appropriate.

5. Remember that piano music is frequently forced, by its own limitations, to rely upon irregular chord formations. Voice parts in these chord progressions need not always be static.

6. Endeavor to retain consistent voice textures for complete phrases. Do not add or subtract notes, because the piano model does so, for no reason other than technical expediency. Retain only those notes that are required for harmonic clarity and that can provide continued voice parts.

Application of these suggestions can, with experience, become constructive habits worthy of cultivation. A single illustration demonstrates their practicality. Point 6, dealing with consistent voice textures, is of special importance when working with piano music as source material. The extent to which inconsistencies of voice textures may appear is well represented in the piano transcription[1] in Example S-47. A comparison of it with the original scoring by Corelli gives some indication of the problems connected with extracting parts with consistent voice textures from piano music.

[1] From the Diller-Quaile *Fourth Solo Book.*

Example S-47

Corelli
Sarabanda

X. OBBLIGATO OR ADDED SECONDARY PARTS ARRANGED FROM HARMONIC PROGRESSIONS

This phase of orchestration is extremely valuable in giving added interest to music which is essentially homophonic. The extraction of independent voice parts from harmonic progressions and their subsequent transformation into secondary voice lines is a direct application of a contrapuntal technique. Examination of the following models will reveal a practical method for arranging these parts.

Example S-48a

Grieg
Album Leaf, Op. 12, No. 7

The three *obbligatos*—[a], [b], and [c]—are in their most elemental form. They were made by starting with *different* chord tones and zigzagging to subsequent chord tones, but differing in direction and design from the original melody whenever possible. The following graphs show the lines of direction.

Example S-48b

In Example S-48c the three counterpoints have rhythmic diversification and movement. They are arranged so that any two can be used in any range with the original melody.

Example S-48c

The principles learned through the study of these models may be applied to any section of the orchestra. Although the method for abstracting these parts may appear to be mechanical, the final results can have interest, vitality, and melodic importance. Example S-49 demonstrates a middle-range *obbligato* scored to come through the full tonal spread.

Example S-49

Reprinted by permission of Edward B. Marks Music Corp., New York; copyright 1944 by Edward B. Marks Music Corp.

XI. ANTIPHONAL EFFECTS

Antiphonal effects may be identified as brief repetitions of fragmentary melodic or rhythmic ideas usually varying in *tessitura* from their source of origin. These echo effects are short canonic imitations which help to develop continuity. They frequently gain coloristic significance and thematic importance in the development of voice parts, especially for full orchestra. A second style of antiphony is that of short answering phrases either in contrasting ranges and/or timbres. Although occasionally used for divided strings, it is a standard device where mixed timbres are available. (See this category in Chaps. 16 and 35.) An effective antiphonal overlapping of a principal melody will be found in the second movement of the Brahms Violin Concerto, starting with the entrance of the solo instrument.

Example S-50

XII. TREMOLO TYPES

Since a detailed study of the technicalities of tremolo types has been made in Chap. 6, further discussion of this subject here is directed toward playing ranges. Interval and chord tremolos in the middle and upper registers of the treble sound well in close position (Examples S-51a, b, and c). Those in the bass register are clearest when set in open position (Examples S-51a and b). Trills can be effectively combined with fingered tremolos, rarely with the bowed style.

Example S-51

Example S-51 (continued)

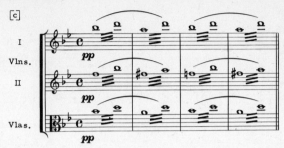

XIII. DANCE FORMS

Dance forms have been included in the *Reference Chart* primarily because of problems arising from the disposition of their characteristic afterbeats. In general, music for most dance forms may be divided structurally into three parts: the melody, the rhythmic afterbeats, and the bass part. As the melody and bass parts rarely require unusual scoring solutions, attention can be directed toward some of the more basic questions concerning the afterbeats.

Chord positions of these rhythmic factors have a direct bearing on the balance of the tonal parts. Detailed study of harmonic progressions in this category shows that second inversions of triads and seventh chords are favored as starting positions for afterbeats. It also reveals that chord progressions take nearest positions and retain a maximum of common

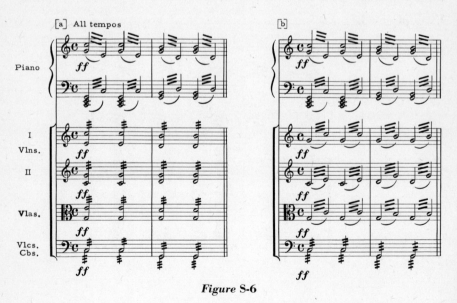

Figure S-6

tones. Obviously, other chord positions are inevitable in progressions but they will be unobtrusive if placed between well-sounding inversions. Close-position chords below those given in Fig. S-6 sound thick and un-wieldy and should be avoided. Consistent chord textures with interlock-ing parts are quite desirable (Fig. S-7). Exceptions to these general practices are fairly common in the more advanced stages of scoring, but they go beyond the scope of practical orchestration.

The concluding examples in this section are devoted to string settings of dance forms. Additional scorings in this classification can now be re-viewed with a revised perception in Examples S-23, S-28, S-30, S-31a and b, S-35, S-39, S-40, S-46a and b, S-47, and S-49.

Figure S-7

Figure S-8

Example S-52

Vivo, ma non troppo

Chopin
Mazurka, Op. 7, No. 2

Example S-53

Albeniz
Sous le palmier (Danse espagnole), Op. 232, No. 3

Example S-54

[a]

Rachmaninov
Valse, Op. 10, No. 2

Example S-54 *(continued)*

Example S-55

Prokofiev
Gavotte, Op. 12, No. 2

Chapter 11

THE WOOD-WIND SECTION

The wood-wind choir is unquestionably the most distinctive section of the orchestra because of its varied timbres, sustaining potentials, and general resourcefulness. When used as a separate unit, its combined timbres blend well together and possess considerable tonal variety, especially when compared with the other sections of the orchestra. When used in conjunction with the strings, entirely new dimensions

appear—melodically, harmonically, and rhythmically. Their use as solo instruments is unmatched since each wood-wind has a distinctive personalized tone. Every solo entrance of an instrument in this section appears as a new character on the scene. Their single and combined effectiveness is practically limitless, yet they do require special consideration because of their fixed timbres and because they vary somewhat according to playing registers. Each division of the section—that is, non-reeds (flutes and piccolo), single reeds (clarinets and saxophones), and double reeds (oboes, English horn, and bassoons)—has a stable tonal color that varies only in matters of intensity (tonal strength) and adaptability (technical capacity).

The problems of intensity are, for the most part, conditioned by playing *tessituras,* that is, the high-medium-low parts of their respective ranges. Their technical capacity (adaptability) varies with each instrument, as does their effectiveness in melodic phrases and rhythmic patterns. Therefore, because of playing registers, it is important that there be an understanding of each instrument's peculiarities of timbre. In brief, the tonal color of each wood-wind remains constant but the intensity of that color can vary. Because of these tonal variations, some thought should be directed toward their place in the general plan of orchestration. As all the wood-winds have a number of points in common, they may be summarized collectively as follows:

1. All tone production is accomplished by means of setting a column of air in motion within a conical or cylindrical tube.[1] The activating means by which this is accomplished becomes a primary factor in establishing the timbre of each instrument. Piccolos and flutes use no reed for this purpose. In this instance, the column of air is set in motion by forcing air from the lips of the player across an opening at the end of the tube. All other wood-winds rely on single or double reeds to generate air-wave activity within the tube of each instrument.

2. The intensity (carrying power or tonal strength) varies with each instrument according to its playing ranges. As a result of this technicality, the extreme upper and lower notes of each instrument are difficult to control in the matters of intonation and dynamics. With this information in mind, it is well to remember that the piccolo, flutes, and clarinets, when used with full orchestra, are not entirely successful when played softly in their extreme upper registers. Conversely, these highest tones can cut through most orchestral textures without forcing. The lowest tones of the flutes and clarinets have unusually fine expressive qualities but are devoid of much tonal strength. Therefore, passages in these *tessituras* should be well exposed; accompaniments should be lightly scored for instruments with a totally different color.

Oboes, bassoons, and the English horn have rather thin, weak tones in their highest registers, while their lowest tones are exactly the opposite in tonal strength. In the hands of inexperienced players, these extremes of range become exceedingly risky, since the intonation dilemma is always present. Even players with considerable experience find it most difficult to control the reeds for *pianissimo* passages on the lowest tones of double-reed instruments. (This problem does not hold true for single-reed instruments.) It is therefore a decided advantage to acquire a working knowledge of the idiosyncrasies of each instrument, so that unnecessary errors of judgment can be avoided.

3. All the wood-wind instruments are comparatively free from technical inadequacies. In the hands of a professional musician, almost any kind of a passage is possible. Yet sound judgment and good taste must be exercised by the orchestrator at all times, lest unidiomatic writing creep into a score, thereby making it musically unsound. In like manner, he must decide on the wisdom of having the oboes or bassoons skip around in sixteenth notes with large interval leaps, when outlining the

[1] The piccolo, flute, and clarinets have a cylindrical tube; the others are conical in shape.

same passage in eighth notes might be a better solution. Needless to say, all these observations are relative, varying in degree according to each player's performing abilities.

4. Each classification of the wood-wind section can be divided into groups corresponding to the approximate ranges of the human voice, as was done for the string section.

Non-reeds	Single Reeds
Piccolo	Clarinet (E♭)
Flute	Clarinet (B♭ and A)
Alto flute	Alto clarinet (E♭)
Bass flute	Bass clarinet (B♭ and A)
Double Reeds	Soprano saxophone (B♭)[1]
Oboe	Alto saxophone (E♭)
English horn (F)	Tenor saxophone (B♭)
Bassoon	Baritone saxophone (E♭)
Contrabassoon	

In this chart, each grouping of instruments of one timbre has been designed to cover four-part writing within its own division. The practice of grouping the wood-wind instruments according to families of one and the same timbre is a distinct help in classifying tonal characteristics, not only of each division of the wood-winds but also for each instrument of the section.

New and special problems, not heretofore encountered, arise in connection with writing for wood-wind instruments. The majority of instruments in this section require *transposition*. Any standard book on the history of orchestral instruments gives the factual background of their origin and explains their development in the technical matters pertaining to the causes for transposition. Suffice it to say that the present state of technical facility and perfection has been reached only after centuries of experimentation and development.

In the matter of transposition for all wind instruments (wood-wind and brass), there are a few fixed points to keep in mind. First, there should be no misunderstanding about the term "transposing." This term is applied to instruments that have a written notation which differs from the sounding notation. In other words, transposed parts become signs for fingering, not signs for pitch.

Transposing instruments came into common practice in order to avoid complicated fingerings resulting from changes of key. Because of this situation, the arranger, not the player, must do the transposing. Inasmuch as the notation for transposing instruments represents signs for fingering

---

[1] Since the mid-twentieth century, this saxophone has become practically obsolete. A second alto saxophone is frequently used as its substitute and/or replacement.

rather than actual pitch, the player of these instruments encounters no new difficulties in changing from a B♭ clarinet to one in A, nor does the performer of an alto saxophone have any problem in changing to any of the other saxophones, since the fingering remains the same for all of them, regardless of voice designation.

The basic formula for determining the interval of transposition for all of the wind instruments (wood-wind and brass) remains constant. In each case the instrument is so constructed that its *lowest* basic tone becomes its *fundamental*. It is from this fundamental that each instrument receives its voice designation, with its natural playing range. All fundamentals may be practical for transposing purposes when compared to middle C. To determine the interval of transposition, count the number of scale degrees from the fundamental—below middle C to middle C. The resulting interval in each case will determine the transposing interval—the notation to be used *above* the sounding note. All wood-wind instruments listed in the previous chart that have no mention of any specific fundamentals are in C and do not require any transposition.

In scoring for the contemporary symphony orchestra, the orchestrator will encounter six degrees of transposition. They are as follows: B♭, A, F, E♭, and two varieties of octave transposition. By applying the general rule for transposition, the intervals of transposition may be summarized by the following groupings:

All B♭ instruments—written a major second higher than they sound.
All A instruments—written a minor third higher than they sound.
All F instruments—written a perfect fifth higher than they sound.
All E♭ instruments—written a major sixth higher than they sound.[1]
All C instruments—sound as written, with a few exceptions.

The two exceptions are the piccolo in C and the contrabassoon. The piccolo in C is written an octave lower than it sounds, while the contrabassoon is written an octave higher than it sounds. In both instances octave transposition was introduced to avoid excessive ledger lines. It should also be noted that the so-called C melody saxophone is a *tenor* instrument and requires a notation one octave higher than it sounds.

A useful point to keep in mind in determining special or exceptional transpositions is that when a wood-wind instrument carries a voice designation in addition to its normal fundamental (tenor, baritone, or bass), it automatically adds *one octave* to its normal transposition. This procedure remains in force just so long as the treble clef is used. A better understanding of the added octave transposition for certain wind instruments may be had by a direct comparison with male voices using the treble clef. All divisions of male voices using the treble clef actually sound one octave lower

[1] The E♭ clarinet is an exception.

than the given notation! This comparison should clarify and establish the reasons for added octaves in the transposition of the bass clarinet and the tenor and baritone saxophones.

The previous sectional chart of wood-wind instruments may now be detailed as follows:

Non-reeds

Piccolo in C—written an octave lower than it sounds.
Flute in C—non-transposing.
Alto flute in G—written a perfect fourth higher than it sounds.

Single Reeds

Clarinet in E♭—written a minor third lower than it sounds.
Clarinet in B♭—written a major second higher than it sounds.
Clarinet in A—written a minor third higher than it sounds.
Alto clarinet in E♭—written a major sixth higher than it sounds.
Bass clarinet in B♭—written a major ninth higher than it sounds.
Bass clarinet in A—written a minor tenth higher than it sounds.[1]
Soprano saxophone in B♭—written a major second higher than it sounds.
Alto saxophone in E♭—written a major sixth higher than it sounds.
Tenor saxophone in B♭—written a major ninth higher than it sounds.
Baritone saxophone in E♭—written an octave plus a major sixth higher than it sounds.

Double Reeds

Oboe—non-transposing.
English horn in F—written a perfect fifth higher than it sounds.
Bassoon—non-transposing.
Contrabassoon—written an octave higher than it sounds.

Many useful deductions can be made from this chart in addition to the listing of transpositions that come under the heading of *specialties*. The alto flute is extremely rare and is to be found only in major orchestras. Its use by composers of all periods has been practically nonexistent. One notable exception is the *Daphnis et Chloé* ballet by Maurice Ravel, which contains at least one exceptionally telling solo passage for this rare instrument. The true bass flute does not appear in any scores of the standard symphonic repertory.

The E♭ clarinet is, to a lesser degree, in the category of unusual orchestral instruments and has been used most infrequently by composers of orchestral music. (It is an integral part of the instrumentation for con-

_____
[1] See the section on The B♭ Bass Clarinet.

cert bands.) In this country, this high, piercing clarinet is generally substituted for the one in D, as scored by Richard Strauss in *Till Eulenspiegel*. A solo use of this instrument may be noted in the last movement
of the *Symphonie fantastique* by Hector Berlioz.

Since the middle of the nineteenth century, English horn solos have almost exclusively been singled out for melodies which are distinctly nostalgic. Such melodies suit the instrument very well, but they by no means
exhaust its full potentialities. Bach's use of the instrument[1] shows that it
can hold its place in carrying on melodies and figurations of all kinds,
while modern composers, notably Hindemith, Prokofiev, and Stravinsky,
not to mention the Americans, Samuel Barber, Aaron Copland, Roy
Harris, and Walter Piston, have shown that it can be used for completely
independent thematic material, with excellent effect. The English-horn
tone is darker and slightly heavier than the oboe, which differences account for its being generally cast in one type of musical expression. It is,
after all, an *alto oboe* and can be treated as such.

The bass clarinet and the contrabassoon have become more or less
regular instruments of the orchestra since the middle 1800s, although the
contrabassoon was used intermittently before that time. The latter three
instruments are to be found in all major orchestras but their use is decidedly restricted in amateur or school groups.

The saxophones, which are the newest members of the wind group,
have become so familiar during the past few decades that they need very
little comment. It should be noted, however, that they have been assid-
uously avoided by the majority of composers of serious symphonic music,
possibly because of their jazz connotations. There is no doubt that the instruments could offer new and unusual possibilities, if exploited with
taste and an understanding of their natural potentials.

Notable examples of good saxophone scoring occur as follows: Alto
saxophone—*L'Arlésienne* Suite by Bizet and the Concertino for Saxophone and Orchestra by Ibert; Tenor saxophone—the suites *Háry János*
by Kodály and *Lt. Kije* by Prokofiev, "The Old Castle" movement from
Pictures at an Exhibition by Moussorgsky (orchestration by Ravel), and
the ballet *Job* by Ralph Vaughan Williams.

[1] Bach and his contemporaries actually wrote for the oboe da caccia, an earlier prototype.

CHART OF RANGES AND TRANSPOSITIONS FOR WOOD-WIND INSTRUMENTS

Figure **W-1**

It will be to every student's advantage to memorize the practical playing ranges of the most commonly used wood-wind instruments. In actual practice this is not as difficult a task as it appears. Non-reeds have approximately the same written range. The ranges of the oboe and English horn are also similar, while that of the bassoon is two octaves lower than the oboe. The written ranges of the stable variety of clarinets are the same, while all the saxophones have a written range which is identical with that of the oboe.

Although originally there were a number of differently pitched clarinets designed for regular use, those in B♭ and A have become universally standardized for orchestra scoring. These two instruments exist for the sole purpose of eliminating awkward keys which, in turn, force unnecessarily awkward fingerings. The proper choice of clarinets—B♭ or A—is dependent then upon the matter of tonality. By way of illustration, consider the following example: If a piece is written in the key of A major, the B♭ instrument (clarinet or trumpet) would be written a major second higher in the key of B major, while A instruments would have the signature for C major. Obviously, the instrument in A would be a better choice in this instance.

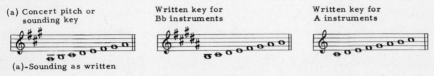

Figure **W-2a**

Pursuing this matter of comparative transpositions, we find that music in the concert key of D♭ (major or its relative minor) would require B♭ instruments to be in the key of E♭ major, while A instruments would be in the key of F♭ major or its more practical enharmonic, E major. The choice in this case would favor instruments in B♭.

Figure **W-2b**

From these two illustrations it can rightfully be deduced that instruments in A are best suited to music in sharp keys, while tonalities in flat keys are most accessible to B♭ instruments. Although some differences of opinion have been expressed by conductors and composers about the tonal differences of B♭ and A clarinets, such differences, if they exist, may be dismissed for all general purposes. However, it should be noted that the A clarinet does have the small-octave C♯ for its last note, which does not exist on the B♭ instrument. It should also be remembered, for those interested in scoring for school orchestras, that clarinets in A are comparatively rare and that it is safer to rely on B♭ instruments.

Direct application of all transpositions for orchestral instruments may be illustrated as follows:

ORCHESTRAL TRANSPOSITIONS

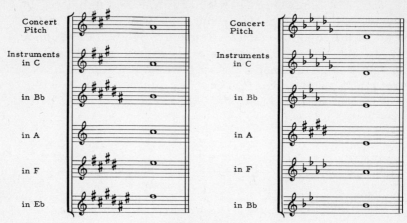

Figure **W-3**

From the above listing of transpositions, it will be clear that no new problems will be encountered in the use of major or minor tonalities; the procedure is the same in both instances.

Chapter 12

THE NON-REEDS

THE FLUTE

(Fr. *flute, grande flute;*
It. *flauto, flauto grande;*
Ger. *Flöte, grosse Flöte*)

Flute
Piccolo

This agile non-reed, originally made of wood but now available in a variety of metals, has practically limitless possibilities both as a solo instrument and in combination with other instruments. Its complete flexibility, technical facility, and general effectiveness make it one of the most useful and dependable of wind instruments. The value of these assets may be realized from a study of its three-octave compass:

1. The lowest octave, starting on middle C, has a tonal quality which is unmatched by any other instrument. A breathy but round, rich tone of genuine poetic beauty best describes these lowest tones, which bear a resemblance to the top notes of a fine contralto voice. However, the notes in this register should not be forced into the strongest dynamics since the tone becomes too breathy and unclear. All important melodic passages in this octave should remain exposed, free from clashes with secondary harmony parts and stronger instrumental timbres.

2. The middle octave is the neutral part of its total range and is less colorful and somewhat lacking in tonal strength. The tone in this octave blends well in chord formations and is well suited to figurations and scale passages of all kinds. Unison doubling with other winds is also satisfactory in this middle register.

3. The highest octave has great brilliance and tonal strength, for once the flute leaves the treble clef and soars upward, its eloquence is assured. Though these top notes can cut through almost any orchestra texture, the tone remains expressively lyric and poetic.

The flute is well suited to all types of scale passages, *arpeggios,* broken chords, and figurations, as well as to solo passages in all styles. Long sustained notes are feasible, but they do not have the same vibrancy as when scored for clarinet or oboe. The following excerpts from standard works have been chosen to illustrate characteristic passages in varying registers:

FLUTE

Example W-1

Beethoven
Symphony No. 3

Stravinsky
Firebird Suite

By permission of J. and W. Chester Ltd., London.

Prokofiev
Peter and the Wolf, Op. 67

By permission of Leeds Music Corp., New York City.

Walter Piston
The Incredible Flutist

THE PICCOLO

(Fr. *petite flute;* It. *flauto piccolo, ottavino;*
Ger. *kleine Flote*)

The piccolo is actually a small flute, being half the size of that instrument, and sounding an octave higher than written. It is generally scored as an interchanging part for either the second or third flute player. When so written, sufficient time should be allowed for the change-over from one instrument to the other.

The piccolo differs from the flute quite radically in the matter of practical playing ranges. Although the curious-minded can find a non-existent middle C for the piccolo in Verdi's *Requiem* (page 214 of the miniature score), along with other notes in its lowest octave, it should be established that the instrument's best playing range begins on two-line C and continues upward for an octave and a sixth. Caution is advised in writing the very highest notes as they are extremely difficult to control and consequently are either always out of tune or come through shrill, strident, and frequently unmusical. These highest tones are practically impossible at a *pianissimo* level, while the lowest octave is of little value in *fortissimo*.

This brilliant little instrument can be effectively used for all passages playable on the flute, but slow, sustained passages sound thin unless doubled in octaves with another wind instrument, and then only for brief moments. The piccolo, when used with two flutes in chord formation, is valuable for increasing a tonal spread in the highest register (see Example W-12).

PICCOLO

Example W-2

By permission of Leeds Music Corp., New York.

Chapter 13

THE SINGLE REEDS

THE Bb AND A CLARINETS

(Fr. *clarinette;* It. *clarinetto;*
Ger. *Klarinette*)

The clarinet of today is the real
prima donna of the wood-winds.
Originally limited in both range

Bb and A Clarinets
Eb Clarinet
Eb Alto Clarinet
Bb Bass Clarinet
The Saxophones

and technical facility, it has become the most versatile of wind instruments since the introduction of the Boehm system of fingering. Its present range of more than three octaves makes it extremely valuable for practically every type of musical expression. Its great versatility makes it indispensable for melodic and chordal writing as well as for *arpeggios,* figurations, and scale passages in almost all tempos and dynamics. In the melodic realm it has a smooth, mellow tone of beauty and expressiveness. Although most orchestrations frequently have the two clarinets playing in the middle range, they are capable of utilizing their complete range without forcing or pinching the tone. A detailed study of the instrument's total range will show that there are some variations in tonal color and intensity.

1. The lowest octave, known as the *chalumeau* register, has an unusually rich, round tone distinctly apart from the other reeds. These tones are unsurpassed for darkly colored solo passages and equally effective when used in a supporting capacity. Although resonant, this octave carries with less intensity than that associated with the upper-middle and high registers and is, therefore, less rewarding when the tone is forced because of heavily scored accompaniments. (See the Introduction to Tchaikovsky's Fifth Symphony.)

2. The notes F to B in the middle octave, comprising the "break" register, are of slightly poorer quality than the others here. They do not

constitute a serious technical difficulty unless used repeatedly in passage work.

3. The penetrating and brilliant tones of the highest octave are a great asset in reinforcing short thematic motives in *tutti* passages where a real cutting-through effect is needed. As these highest tones are somewhat difficult to control, they are not recommended as chord notes in the softer dynamics. The top four semitones are rather dangerous for inexperienced players. The examples that follow illustrate some typical clarinet passages.

CLARINET

Example W-3

Example W-3 *(continued)*

THE E♭ AND E♭ ALTO CLARINETS

Since neither of these instruments has become a standard part of symphonic instrumentation, no detailed analysis will be undertaken here. Both instruments are essentially part of the wind sections of symphonic and military bands.

THE B♭ BASS CLARINET

(Fr. *clarinette basse;* It. *clarinetto basso, clarone;*
Ger. *Bassklarinette*)

The bass clarinet occupies the same position in the clarinet family that the cello does in the string section. It remained infrequently used until the middle of the nineteenth century, when it figured prominently in the works of Wagner, Strauss, and Mahler. Its slightly muffled but evocative timbre, first employed sparingly for relatively short lyrical passages, has been turned, in more recent decades, to startlingly original figurations which emphasize its technical agility and versatility. Twentieth-century composers have replaced the former mournful melodies and occasional chordal bass passages by bringing these new effects into prominence.

Nevertheless, successful writing for this instrument requires a thorough understanding of its potential strength and weakness. Essentially, it is of the same technical facility as the standard clarinets and is capable of playing the same type of passage. However, extra consideration must be given to its normal lowest register. The difficulty is to attain and maintain clarity for any fast-moving parts in the lowest range. While all variations of dynamics are possible, *fortissimo* parts sound forced and rather unmusical. Actually, the moderately loud-to-soft dynamics fare best and should be well exposed, since the bass clarinet does not have great tonal strength.

It is essentially a *solo* instrument, excellent when used as the bass part for wood-wind chords and effective for short, swirling scale passages, broken chords, and figurations. **Note:** Its tones are less clear than the bassoon in identical ranges.

For many years it was common practice to write parts for the bass clarinet in the bass clef. Originally there was also an instrument in A as well as in B♭, but in recent years the A instrument has disappeared and all parts are now written in the treble clef.

BASS CLARINET

Example W-4a

By permission of C. F. Peters Corporation, 373 Fourth Ave., New York, N.Y.

Example W-4b

By permission of C. F. Peters Corporation, 373 Fourth Ave., New York, N.Y.

Example W-4c

Copyright 1921 by Edition Russe de Musique. Copyright assigned 1947 to Boosey and Hawkes Ltd. Used by permission.

THE SAXOPHONES

(Fr. *saxophone;* It. *saxofono, sassofono;* Ger. *Saxophon*)

The saxophones are a homogeneous group of single-reed instruments that have not as yet been accepted as regular members into the family of orchestral sections. Although the E♭ and B♭ tenor instruments have been used occasionally in symphonic scores (see discussion of saxophone scoring in Chap. 11), the section as a whole seems destined for parts designed for school orchestras and symphonic or military bands. One could argue that the omission of these instruments as a regular part of a symphonic wind section is unfortunate because the saxophones have tonal qualities unmatched by the other winds. To a degree this reasoning is sound and perhaps accounts for saxophones being used occasionally as a special instrument. It is wise to write such passages so that they can be played by one of the clarinetists, since most players double on these single-reed instruments.

There need be little said about the timbre of the saxophone since its constant use in dance bands and show music has made it the most familiar of wind instruments. It possesses great flexibility, tonal range, and sustaining qualities at all speeds and dynamics. Perhaps its most useful function at present is in substituting for various missing instruments in school orchestras. In this connection the practice is serviceable, especially in playing cues for oboe, bassoon, and horn. If played with a minimum of *vibrato,* saxophones need not destroy the equilibrium of symphonic timbres.

Although six varieties of saxophones exist, only some three or four have become more or less standardized. Music for symphonic bands includes parts for two altos, one tenor, and one baritone saxophone. Most dance and show scores omit the baritone.

The chart shown in Fig. W-4 gives the written and playing ranges of the saxophones.

(a) These notes are missing from some instruments.

Figure W-4

Although the saxophones in this survey are being considered as supplementary instruments, some practical suggestions for their scoring are being discussed as a separate division of the wood-wind section. In setting four-part music for these instruments, little difficulty will be encountered since there are no timbre problems. Furthermore, there is no necessity for opening up close-position chords; saxophones sound well in all close-position chord progressions. The following setting is for one each of this group.

Example W-5

Since the soprano instrument seems to be disappearing from general use and is being supplemented by a second alto, the arrangement for four-part music, omitting the soprano and substituting the second alto, would be as follows:

Soprano—first alto	Tenor—tenor
Alto—second alto	Bass—baritone

From purely technical considerations, the scoring for saxophones is not radically different from the scoring for any of the other wood-winds. Their range designations (soprano, alto, tenor, baritone) furnish the clues to their usual playing *tessituras*. They have no problematical timbre or technique limitations that might require unusual attention. They blend well together and with other instruments. The use of saxophones in a symphonic score must, in the final analysis, be left to the discrimination of the orchestrator.

Chapter 14

THE DOUBLE REEDS

THE OBOE

(Fr. *hautbois;* It. *oboe;*
Ger. *Oboe, Hoboe*)

| |
| Oboe |
| English Horn |
| Bassoon |
| Contrabassoon |

The oboe is, without doubt, the
most distinctive instrument of the
wood-wind group. Its plaintive yet penetrating voice carries surprisingly
well through most string and wind accompaniments, providing that a
suitable balance exists. Its tonal qualities are particularly well suited to
melodic phrases that are nostalgically expressive, poignant, or sadly
pathetic. In a word, the tone is *fragile*.

While it can change its tune to one of rustic gaiety and merriment, its
fixed penetrating timbre cannot be changed. It can be modified somewhat by unison or octave playing with other winds or strings. (Examples:
Unison playing—first theme, first movement of Schubert's *Unfinished*
Symphony; Octave playing—slow movement of Schumann's Fourth
Symphony.) Its fixed-timbre focus is especially important when scoring
the oboe as part of wood-wind chords. Choose chord tones that can best
stand emphasis.

Although most scale passages and figurations are possible on this
instrument, large interval skips in fast tempos are risky. The oboe is
essentially a *lyric* instrument and should be scored as such. While rapid
broken chords or *arpeggios* are not idiomatic for oboes, rapidly repeated
notes, in chord formations with other winds, are decidedly effective. (See
opening measures of Mendelssohn's *Italian* Symphony.) Important short
figurations and long sustained notes have a special interest when played
on the oboe.

Its entire playing range requires extra attention and clarification. The
first four semitones of the lowest octave are very risky for all but professional players. These notes are usually insecure and of poor intona-

147

tion. The remainder of the octave is practical for all melodic and harmonic writing that is idiomatic and characteristic of the instrument. The top octave and a third is the instrument's best playing range from every consideration. The tone in this spread is slightly less reedy than in the lower octave and is excellent for expressive melodies of all styles. The tone does begin to thin out and become less expressive, however, as the highest notes are reached. The last four semitones in the top register are decidedly insecure for the unskilled player.

OBOE

Example W-6

Example W-6 *(continued)*

Prokofiev
Classical Symphony

THE ENGLISH HORN

(Fr. *cor anglais;* It. *corno inglese;* Ger. *englisch Horn*)

The English horn is capable of great expressiveness but has somewhat limited playing potentialities. As used by Bach, it was of equal rank with the oboe and bassoon, but it fell into disuse at the end of the Baroque period. Starting with Haydn and continuing on to Brahms, it is conspicuously absent from scores. Not until the middle of the nineteenth century did composers of program music become interested in its peculiarly fragile and nostalgic qualities and revive it as an integral part of their instrumentation. Twentieth-century composers have shown that the English horn can be successfully adapted to new and expanded idiomatic playing potentials, devoid of sentimentality, without losing sight of the instrument's limited versatility. This newer conception includes repetitions of short melodic phrases and *ostinatos,* pastoral-like figurations with independence of melodic line and lyrical passages. English horn parts can have the same fluidity as the oboe and bassoon.

Although the playing range of the English horn has approximately the same written range as the oboe, its highest octave has been generally excluded since the tone here is thin as compared to the oboe in the same register. Its rich, alto sonority is best suited to sustained melodic passages of poetic beauty that can be played in the medium-soft dynamics. It is not particularly effective in the louder dynamic levels and has generally been omitted from *tuttis* for this reason. Parts for this instrument are usually written so that they can be played interchangeably by the second or third oboist. The two bottom octaves provide the best playing range. Very rapid figurations, though technically possible, are not unqualifiedly successful and are therefore rarely included. Since its tonal strength does not exceed a comfortable *forte,* harmonic accompaniments for it should be thinly scored with contrasting timbres. The English horn is essentially an instrument with rather definite dynamic limitations that should not be ignored or overlooked if it is to remain in character.

The following representative passages illustrate the unique place of this highly specialized instrument.

ENGLISH HORN

Example W-7

Copyright 1901/29 by Breitkopf and Hartel. With permission of Breitkopf and Hartel, Wiesbaden.

Copyright 1921 by Edition Russe de Musique.
Copyright assigned 1947 to Boosey and Hawkes Ltd. Used by permission.

THE BASSOON

(Fr. *basson;* It. *fagotto;* Ger. *Fagott*)

The bassoon, actually a bass oboe, has been referred to as "the clown of the orchestra." However, like every good clown, it is very versatile, as a close study of its playing potentials will reveal. It uses two clefs (bass and tenor), the latter being reserved for parts that would otherwise require many ledger lines. Because of its predominately low playing registers, scoring becomes clearer through an understanding of its varying range differences.

1. Its lowest octave has full, round tones that serve as excellent bass notes for wind chords. Melodic phrases in this range create an atmosphere of austere, dark melancholy, which is completely unique in orchestral sonorities. Tchaikovsky felt and understood the brooding color of this range very well, as exemplified by the opening measures of his *Pathétique* Symphony. Study of this passage also shows the wisdom of keeping all thematic material well exposed, since the tonal strength in this octave is not sufficient to carry over a thick accompaniment. Many composers have exploited the droll humor of this low register for tunes of the *scherzo* variety. Mozart made great use of it in his many operas. One of the most striking illustrations is the main theme of Dukas' *L'Apprenti sorcier.* Broken chords, broken octaves, and general passage work are all possible in the moderate tempos. (See Haydn's *Military* Symphony.) **Note:** The lowest four semitones are difficult to control in *pianissimo.*

2. The strong reedy quality and the intensity of the lowest octave are less pronounced in the middle-octave range. Nevertheless, melodic passages in this compass have considerable expressiveness and, as used by Sibelius in his Fifth Symphony, assume new unearthly and mysterious shades of color heretofore unexplored by most composers of abstract music.

3. The top octave is the tenor range of the bassoon and has a plaintive, almost wailing quality which is excellent for slow-moving melodies that are poignantly expressive. The tone here is thin and will not be heard with heavy accompaniments. Igor Stravinsky used these top notes with extraordinary effect in the opening measures of his *Le Sacre du printemps,* a passage which never ceases to cause consternation among bassoonists. This top octave is comparatively weak and thin, somewhat like the falsetto of a tenor voice, and its highest notes are extremely risky for all but professional players.

In the writing of bassoon parts, as with all the wood-winds, a balance between melodic ideas and their harmonic counterparts can be achieved only by spacing these elements so that the forward motion of the principal part does not come into conflict with the secondary parts. The answer to this problem lies in the proper evaluation of the comparative sonorities of melodic and harmonic textures. The bassoons have good blending qualities that are often useful in scores which call for two horns instead of the usual four. Triads and four-voiced chords, when scored for bassoons and horns, have the effect of full-horn sonority. Interlocking these instruments in chord progressions has a neutralizing effect.

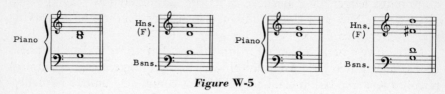

Figure W-5

BASSOON

Example W-8

Reprinted by permission of Durand and Cie, Paris, copyright owners, Elkan-Vogel Co., Inc., Philadelphia, Pa., Agents.

By permission of Boosey-Hawkes, Inc., New York and London.

THE CONTRABASSOON

(Fr. *contrebasson;* It. *contrafagotto;* Ger. *Kontrafagott)*

The contrabassoon occupies the same place in the wood-wind section as the contrabass in the string section. It is the least versatile of the wood-winds and its use is something of a rarity. Passages for this rather unwieldy instrument may be found in the Finales of Beethoven's Fifth and Ninth Symphonies as well as in the final movement of Brahms's First Symphony. Richard Strauss used its heavy, ponderous tones to good effect in a number of his symphonic poems, notably in *Death and Transfiguration.* Its potentialities for droll humor are effectively realized in *L'Apprenti sorcier* by Dukas and the "Beauty and the Beast" movement of Ravel's *Ma Mère l'oye* Suite.

Since the reed of this instrument vibrates very slowly, comparable to 16-foot pedal tones of an organ, and requires exceptional breath control on the part of the player, it is advisable to avoid extra-rapid passages and notes of unusually long duration. The contrabassoon's chief asset is in reinforcing the bass-part wind chords in much the same way as the double basses do for the strings and the tubas for the brass. Short solo passages, though rare, can be effective if they are of short duration. Finally, it is an instrument found only in major orchestras and its general use is therefore limited.

CONTRABASSOON

Example W-9

Reprinted by permission of Durand and Cie, Paris, copyright owners, Elkan-Vogel Co., Inc., Philadelphia, Pa., agents.

Chapter 15

SCORING THE WOOD-WINDS
AS AN INDEPENDENT SECTION

As has been stated, the wood-winds are divided into homogeneous groupings (non-reeds, single reeds, and double reeds), with each division having instruments that are constructed in differing ranges approximating the tonal ranges of the human voice. With

Divided Homogeneous
  Groupings
Mixed Timbres
Tonal Balance
Chord Spacings
Structural Expansions

this in mind, it is possible to consider the practical over-all tonal range of each separate group in terms of its high, medium, and low playing compass. This kind of instrumental thinking helps to determine the best playing ranges for each instrument within the various groups.

Several preliminary exercises are necessary before instrumental thinking of this kind can be practiced with assurance. Orchestration, as an art, recognizes the necessity for blended timbres, as well as their functional positions in the texture of good part writing. The uniformity of timbres, as found in the string section, does not exist in the wind section, which is one of mixed timbres. Therefore, the orchestrator must be constantly alert for these color differences so that a proper balance of timbres can be achieved. It should also be remembered that these very timbre differences can give distinctive tonal definition to any voice in all part writing. By scoring *America* in its usual four-part harmonization, some basic observations can be made resulting from the juxtaposition of different timbres. The common practice of giving the highest part to a flute and assigning the other parts in the order of their appearance on the score page produces the following result.

Example W-10a

America

The weakness of this scoring lies in the poor tonal distribution of the soprano and alto parts. Whenever mixed timbres occur, care must be taken to assure clear tonal definition of the melodic line. In Example W-10a, the low flute and the lower oboe cannot give this clarity. The stronger oboe timbre would dominate the flute in this register.

Two alternatives are possible in order to adjust this poor tonal balance. The first and most obvious one would be to invert the flute and oboe parts so that the latter would then be playing the soprano part. The second and more effective alternative calls for rearranging the voice parts in open position without changing the *tessitura* of the bass part. This can be accomplished by raising the melody an octave and inverting the alto and tenor parts. The new setting will give greater clarity and resonance to each part and also provide better playing *tessituras* for each instrument.

Example W-10b

With the flute *above* the staff for the complete melody, the part will have the right tonal strength to carry well in the open-position progressions. There is also better voice leading in the two inside parts and a larger spread is provided between the flute and oboe parts.

A comparative analysis of these two settings of *America* offers rather conclusive proof of the need for understanding the importance of chord spacing, especially when mixed timbres are involved. Because each of the four instruments has special and varying tonal characteristics, each must be placed in its best playing range with spacings determined by the timbres of the adjacent instruments.

Scoring for wood-winds in pairs necessitates the expansion of four-voice chorals by the addition of harmonic fillers and octave doublings. If the new eight-voice arrangement is given to the wood-winds in their normal order (high to low), the setting would be as follows:

Example W-11a

The following deductions can be made from the foregoing example: (1) Single stems for two parts on the same staff may be used providing both parts have the same rhythmic patterns. (2) The first flute and the second oboe have the melody in octaves. (3) The octave-bassoon part is desirable as a support to the upper six voices. (4) The instrumental timbres have not been overlapped.

The next setting shows an interlocking of timbres in the oboe and clarinet parts. This device is useful inasmuch as it tends to blend the affected parts by neutralizing their identities as blocked sonorities. **Note:** Practically all *tutti* wood-wind chords use this arrangement whenever feasible; the deciding factor is always that of tonal range spread. The better blending of voices that is achieved by this method makes it preferable to the former example.

Example W-11b

A final wood-wind setting of *America* calls for a voice structure of twelve parts. It will be noted that the oboe and clarinet parts show an overlapping, as in the previous example, but that greater freedom of voice leading in these two parts is now possible because of the greater number of total voices. The importance of good voice leading cannot be overstressed in dealing with instruments of varying timbres, since their equally varying tonal intensities require the utmost care in arranging them so that they will sound well in each division of the wind section. Wood-wind parts should not be arbitrarily arranged according to blocked-chord progressions. Rather, they should be arranged so that each instrument of the section moves as an independent voice—yet always in conjunction with and regulated by the voice leading of the other instruments of the section.

Example W-12

TWELVE PARTS

Chapter 16

THE REFERENCE CHART OF KEYBOARD IDIOMS AND PATTERNS APPLIED TO THE WOOD-WIND SECTION

Previous application of the *Reference Chart* to the string section demonstrated the necessity for making certain structural changes before attempting any actual scoring. These changes can, for the most part, be applied equally well to settings for the wood-winds as an independent unit, providing that suitable provisions are made for differences in ranges, timbres, and tonal strengths and weights.

The résumés given for each of the wood-winds indicated their tonal characteristics. It is this area of tonal differences that offers a challenge to the orchestrator, for the selection of a wood-wind for any given phrase or passage should not be governed solely by its playing range. Rather, each instrument should be selected according to its total tonal potentials: range, timbre, and intensity. In each instance, the means for the full representation of musical values is paramount.

The quality of *appropriateness* may be evaluated by a comparison of the flute, oboe, and clarinet within a specific range. All three instruments have an ascending two-octave compass starting on middle C, yet they will vary considerably in this compass in tonal strength, definition, and intensity. The tonal profile of any musical idea within this range will therefore be affected by the timbre of the instrument selected—non-reed, single, or double reed.

As one means of orchestral contrast is achieved by the juxtaposition of sectional timbres, a scoring technique for the wood-winds as an independent unit becomes an invaluable asset. Following the format used for the strings, this can be approached progressively through the application of the *Reference Chart*. Differences between the scoring for the two mediums will thus become identified as definite idiomatic peculiarities and characteristics which can then be adjusted to meet the requirements of appropriateness for each phrase or passage.

I. BROKEN INTERVALS

Wood-wind scorings of broken intervals, in all categories, may follow the structural patterns previously established for the strings. Literal transcription for single instruments is often possible because of their remarkable agility and comparative freedom from intonation irregularities. Difficulties in this instance will be in proportion to the size of the intervals. The deciding factors—tempos, ranges, and dynamics—will remain constant.

One specific idiomatic difference between the strings and the wood-winds is to be noted. Repeated single notes for wood-winds are neither practical nor effective, except for short passages. Broken intervals having extended note repetitions are therefore generally to be avoided. Complete intervals, in a non-*legato* style, may be played as divided, repeated notes in two or more parts. For a *legato* phrasing, a single slurred part paired with the rhythmic repeated notes will suffice. Broken intervals divided for two instruments with the same basic timbres retain tonal continuity while those with mixed timbres will vary in color and intensity.

Example W-13

Example W-13 *(continued)*

II. BROKEN CHORDS

Only slight structural changes will be necessary for wood-wind adaptations of the models in this classification previously scored for strings.

Some slight variations in harmonic spacings may be needed as a result of the inequality of tonal balance within the section. This element is an especially delicate one in establishing contrast between the melody and harmony without overstraining the player's capacities in maintaining good breath control.

Wood-wind chords require considerable tonal evaluation if an improper note emphasis is to be avoided. Here, the factors of timbres and tonal strengths help to determine the best playing positions. These conditions are relative, being dependent upon the context and variety of instrumental combinations.

Only those models in the *Reference Chart* which can be idiomatically transcribed have been included in this classification. Excluded excerpts may be used for orchestral scoring where the wood-wind writing becomes radically different from that demonstrated in this chapter.

1. Left-hand Broken Chords in Close Position

Example W-14

This scoring retains the voice parts used in Example S-8. The inside clarinets have good contrast with the oboe melody.

Example W-15

The pairing of the flute and oboe is standard procedure for octaves in this range. It is superior in timbre blending to octaves arranged in a single timbre. The alternating clarinets are given, to show the way parts may be divided for long passage work. The second bassoon is used as extra bass support for the octave melody.

Example W-16

Mozart
Sonata No. 3

Example W-16a *(continued)*

Example W-16b *(continued)*

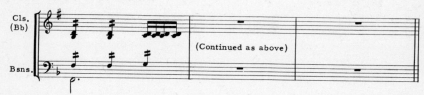

The *forte* dynamic here suggests a *tutti* scoring with a maximum of sonority. The version given at [b] gives the chord structure as non-*legato* repeated notes.

2. Left-hand Broken Chords in Open Position

Example W-17

Brahms
Sonata, Op. 5

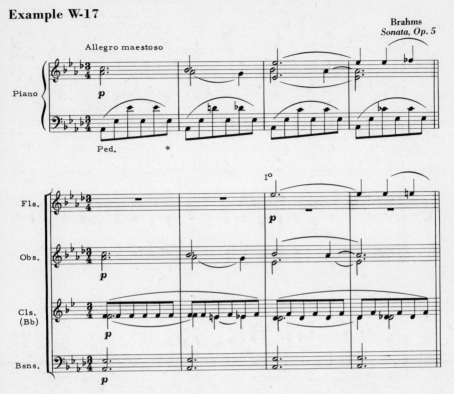

The descending chromatic line emerging from the repeated E's in the clarinets establishes the rhythmic pattern for the whole passage. The fifths in the bassoons have sufficient tonal strength to support the treble parts.

Example W-18

Full rhythmic chords covering the middle register, coupled with the repeated octave in the bassoons, provide maximum support for the strong treble parts. The phrasing for the latter keeps the *staccato* sixteenths within each phrase grouping (1).

3. Broken Chords Spaced for Two Hands

Example W-19a

This setting is a good illustration of the structural idiomatic differences to be encountered with string and wood-wind scorings of identical models. (Compare with Example S-14.) The double reeds here provide harmonic continuity for the first three measures, while the less pungent flutes and clarinets carry out the rhythmic figuration. The scoring of the canonic entrances, starting in measure five, and the subsequent chord positions are important details for study.

Example W-19b

Although this excerpt could conceivably be scored as given in Examples S-15b and c, it is more in character for wood-winds as a two-part dialogue without sustained parts.

4. Broken Chords in Right Hand with Implied Melodic Line

Example W-20

Example W-20 *(continued)*

The implied melodic lines of the first four measures in the double reeds will project beyond the antiphonal triplets in the flutes and clarinets. Dividing the melodic line, starting in measure six, is a technical expedient favoring the player and increasing tonal variety.

5. Broken Chords with Blocked Melodic and Rhythmic Patterns

The wood-winds, as an independent unit, are not well adapted to chords in this classification, as the rhythmic patterns cannot be idiomatically maintained except as repeated notes (Example S-17). Representative models of chordal repetitions include the opening measures of the *Italian* Symphony by Mendelssohn and the symphonic poem *Don Juan* by Strauss. However, limited sequences of blocked chords are playable if arranged as given for the following Weber excerpt.

Example W-21

6. Arpeggiated Chords

Arpeggiated chords, essentially diatonic and free from successive repeated notes, are quite common for flute and clarinet in a variety of tempos. They are less satisfactory for the double reeds unless restricted to short passages in the slower tempos.

Chords in this category have their greatest effect when scored for the complete section (bassoons usually excluded), with full orchestra. Unison doublings with strings is ineffective and impractical. Yet sectional scoring of these chords in contrary motion has been employed by many composers since first introduced by Richard Wagner.

Following are two short extracts showing divided parts for these chords.

Example W-22

III. MELODIC LINES AND FIGURATIONS

In selecting instruments for melodic lines and figurations, the orchestrator must weigh not only musical values but technical considerations as well. The string player is always subject to the accuracy of finger positions and bow control. The wood-wind player must coordinate a manual technique with reed, lip, and breath control. As a result, tone quality is quite variable, being dependent upon the player's training and experience. Awkward fingerings for complicated passages tend to accentuate mental hazards, thus affecting both intonation and tone quality.

1. Large Melodic Skips

Melodies with large intervals are often the source of tonal insecurity. The degree of difficulty varies with each instrument and with each player. The following fugal subject by Stravinsky illustrates this element of relativity.

Example W-23

By permission of Boosey-Hawkes, Inc., New York and London.

This unaccompanied theme for oboe, with its chromatically altered intervals, serves to focus attention on the importance of planning practical orchestration within certain rather specific technical limits. It likewise permits comparative evaluations of playing techniques.

Each reader can decide how this theme would sound if played by a nonprofessional oboist. Yet, if performed by an experienced but nonprofessional flutist or clarinetist, reasonably good tonal accuracy could be expected. This comparison is intended to clarify the differences in tonal production between the single- and double-reed instruments. Control of double reeds is especially precarious for all but the best players, which fact should not be overlooked in finding appropriate settings for melodies in this category. Other considerations of tempo, range, and dynamic level also figure as extenuating factors.

These considerations have been taken into account in the scoring of Example W-24. Although the melody would have more definition if scored for an oboe, there would be some intonation risks unless played by a good technician. If this excerpt had the same structural plan of Example S-23, the oboe could then be given the highest voice part. The wood-wind setting here is both adequate and practical. The clarinets, as arranged at (1), demonstrate how repeated intervals can be played *legato* by contrary motion in the same divided part.

Example W-24

Grieg
Waltz, Op. 38, No. 7

In summation: Piccolo, flutes, and clarinets are best suited to figurations with large and irregular intervals; double reeds, less flexible but possible, in slowed-down or augmented notations.

Some forms of melodic lines in this category fare better when arranged in two parts, as previously recommended for the strings.

Example W-25a

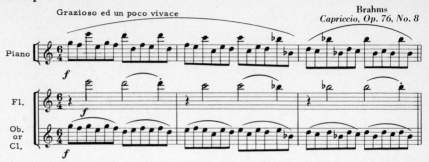

Divided melodies in this form gain considerably in clarity and sonority, especially when used with full orchestra, and they are particularly convenient in rapid tempos. Melodic implications assume greater clarity when the extracted highest part is placed in a stronger timbre than its rhythmic counterpart.

Example W-25b

2. Outlining a Melodic Line

The principle of extracting definitive parts from a figuration, as given in Fig. W-6 and Example W-26, is the same one used for outlining a melodic line. This method generally places the strongest wind instrument on the extracted, less rhythmic part. This device renders its best effect with full orchestra, being less useful in sectional scoring.

Figure W-6

Example W-26

3. Dividing a Melodic Line

As previously noted (Example S-28), melodic lines may not only be divided to avoid awkward intervals, but also to complete and augment part writing. It is a device singularly felicitous for wood-winds, where contrasting timbres can enhance the tonal variety of a two-part dialogue.

Example W-27

4. Melodic Lines Combined with Repeated Notes

Repeated single notes are not idiomatic for the wood-wind choir unless they are an integral part of the voice writing as given in Example W-28. Here, note repetitions are not employed as auxiliary, rhythmic expedients; rather they function as an equal voice in a quasi-contrapuntal progression. The soprano and tenor parts in the same timbre will have good contrast with the secondary parts in the clarinets.

Example W-28

Mendelssohn
Song without Words, Op. 67, No. 5

5. Melodic Settings: Contrasts, Comparative Strengths, and Repeated Phrases

This classification requires good judgment based on the subtleties of instrumental timbres and tonal intensities. The orchestrator is free to choose instrumental colorings for blending potentials in their most favorable positions. In each instance instrumental timbres should become more or less synonymous with musical values. Tonal profile or definition depends, to a large degree, not only on the solo melody part, but also on its contrast with the surrounding secondary parts.

These tenets of musical values should be observed. The objectives are those of balance and blending of mixed timbres. It is essential that tonal weights, resulting from timbre overlapping, be arranged for the best sounding position of chord progressions. The two following passages, with similar harmonizations, illustrate the wide latitude that is possible with chord settings.

Example W-29

Repeated phrases are excellent material for promoting contrast when scored with mixed timbres. Such phrases may be literal transcriptions or short canonic imitations arranged antiphonally. However, phrases so employed require subtle reflections of dynamic levels.

Two phrase sequences in Schubert's *Unfinished* Symphony provide good source material for the clarification of this point. In both instances the phrase repetitions start *forte* and progress toward a tonal fade-out. The first exposition has this sequence ending with an oboe ("*ppp*"), while the second one ends with a flute ("*pp*"). In both, the timbre juxtaposition has effective contrast, but the first is less satisfactory than the second because of the heavier tonal weight of the oboe, notwithstanding its dynamic marking. A flute or a clarinet can accomplish this ending more successfully.

Example W-30

Still another and more pronounced example of timbre juxtaposition occurs just before the development section in the first movement of Tchaikovsky's *Pathétique* Symphony. The blending process here is never quite realized, which accounts for most conductors substituting a bass clarinet for the last four notes in the bassoon. From the dynamics it is evident that the composer recognized these timbre discrepancies.

Example W-31

6. Nonmetrical Passages

Nonmetrical or quasi-cadenza passages are best when confined to a single solo part. This classification, as used here, refers to uneven note groupings that are not an integral part of the regular metrical divisions of the notation. It does *not* refer to grace notes.

IV. IMPLIED BASS PARTS

No new technique is involved in working with this category for the wood-winds. It is a device which is rarely necessary for this choir, except for those times when extended part writing is required.

V. SINGLE-NOTE, INTERVAL, AND CHORD REPETITIONS

The findings made for the strings with these phases of scoring apply equally well to the wood-winds with very little change.

1. Repeated Notes—without Rests

Example W-32

Here, the bassoon is given a maximum of contrast with the treble parts while the repeated notes are confined to the lightest flute timbre.

2. Repeated Notes—with Rests

Example W-33

A literal transcription of the note-rest pattern has been discarded in favor of a more idiomatic adaptation giving full chordal representation on each full beat.

3. Interval and Chord Repetitions

Intervals and chords which occur with notations resembling afterbeats constitute a special category in orchestral scoring. When the rhythmic part falls within metrical divisions in each measure, such parts may be regarded as afterbeats and may be scored accordingly. However, if this notation occurs within a measure having but a single pulsation or strong beat, as in Example W-34, the part will become more playable if scored as repeated notes with full metric representation.

Example W-34

The following examples are drawn from alternating hand patterns. They are repeated here for the wood-winds so that direct comparisons can be made with the previous settings for strings (Examples S-35, S-36, and S-37). Only two observations are pertinent. In Example W-36a, the implied chords on the weak beats of each measure have been assigned to the heavier double reeds. In Example W-36b, the problem of the repeated F♯ has been circumvented by writing it as an embellished part.

Example W-35

Example W-36a

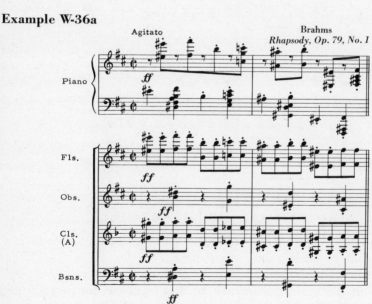

Example W-36b

VI. TWO- AND THREE-PART MUSIC

The approach to scoring two- and three-part music for the wood-winds has somewhat different values than those used for the strings. These changed values are due mainly to the heterogeneous character of the section as a unit and each instrument's natural proclivity for solo playing.

Mixed timbres, within the section, favor part writing rather than chordal progressions. These distinctions form the core of idiomatic characteristics for determining details of structural textures. The place of harmonic fillers as added voice parts must be determined in accordance with each specific passage in its full context.

Symphonic composers since Haydn and Mozart have relied upon short two- and three-part wood-wind passages as a means of securing contrast. Their effectiveness lies in the juxtaposition of timbres and the number of voice parts. Latter-day composers have continued this format, varying the tonal spreads of the wood-winds in proportion to the general fullness of the orchestral texture.

1. Homophonic

Examination of the musical examples used for this classification indicates the advisability of using a minimum of added parts. Their inclusion remains the orchestrator's prerogative which, in the final analysis, can be judged only through an appraisal of the amount and kind of sonority that is desirable. The following settings, Examples W-37, W-38a and W-38b, have been arranged to show the directions possible for idiomatic voice expansions in this category. Example W-38b illustrates outlining within the section (oboe part).

Example W-37

Example W-38

The transcription for Example W-39 is not arbitrary; only the *texture* should remain intact. In this instance the double reeds were selected because of their archaic timbre connotations, the flute octave being optional.

Example W-40 illustrates the value of harmonic fillers if used with an extended melodic range. The two flutes and second clarinet chords form a center, neutral block which does not interfere with either the high-octave melody or the tenor-range counterpoint.

Example W-39

Beethoven
Minuetto, Op. 49, No. 2

Example W-40

Joseph Wagner
Hudson River Legend

Reprinted by permission of Edward B. Marks Music Corp., New York; copyright 1944 by Edward B. Marks Music Corp.

2. Polyphonic

Generalities established for this classification in the string section apply equally well here. Literal transcription is often possible, providing that theme subjects can be carried through in their entirety in one instrument. Entrances of subject matter should have the advantages of contrasting timbres whenever possible.

Example W-41

J. S. Bach
Fugue No. 1

Example W-41 *(continued)*

The exposition of this C major Fugue from Bach's *Well-tempered Clavichord* emphasizes some of the problems confronting the orchestrator of music in this classification. Phrase markings, especially in the works of Bach, are either nonexistent or the work of an editor. In either case, they must be adjusted to fit the idiomatic playing techniques of each wood-wind. This setting has been arranged to have each fugal entrance in a contrasting timbre, thus necessitating the premature entrance of the flute in the third measure to space the clarinet properly for its second entrance in measure four. The part writing should be kept flexible enough to insure adequate readjustment of details in this variety.

3. Style Mixtures

Wood-wind scorings of style mixtures follow the same general patterns established for each respective category. It is a phase of scoring which allows considerable leeway for ingenuity and inventiveness on the part of the orchestrator.

Example W-42

Example W-42 *(continued)*

VII. SPACING PROBLEMS IN THE MIDDLE REGISTER

1. Large Harmonic Gaps

This classification has, as its first requisite, the proper rearrangement of structural elements for the purpose of establishing part writing for instruments rather than literal adaptations of patterns devised as keyboard music. Piano music in particular must, of necessity, frequently resort to figurations which are within an octave but which place the hands far apart in the treble and bass registers in order to secure a maximum of contrast and sonority. These passages must be rearranged so that their musical values are preserved, yet reset for idiomatic use by various instrumental combinations. Once these changes have been made, decisions concerning the selection of suitable instrumental timbres can be carried out with greater understanding of the problems involved. Short score models illustrating the method of resetting these elements are given under this classification for full orchestra.

2. Sustained Notes, Intervals, and Chords

Sustained notes, intervals, and chords are resonance factors which are to be evaluated according to the musical context of each passage. Their usage is variable, being dependent upon structural considerations and tonal balance. They are distinctive harmonic devices useful for establishing chordal coherence and are natural counterparts of homophonic music. Their number and strength usually vary in proportion to each entire tonal spread. Piano music, with its keyboard limitations, is handicapped in this particular respect since *sostenuto,* of any significant duration, is not a successful adjunct of piano resonance. It remains for the orchestrator to evaluate this negative characteristic in planning the structural arrangement of pianistic passages. Sustained notes or intervals in the middle registers can be invaluable, yet they should not be employed arbitrarily or indiscriminately. Their place as a structural element can be progressively traced in models employing this form of harmonic continuity.

VIII. CONTRAST PROBLEMS CONDITIONED BY DYNAMICS

Dynamic variation automatically suggests complementing variation of tonal spreads as well as gradations of tonal weights. Well-planned juxtapositions of these elements can be one means of securing contrast in a variety of textures and ranges. The orchestrator's task here is to achieve a good balance between these details as they occur in progression.

Ordinarily, passages with the stronger dynamics gain in contrast and sonority when expanded in tonal range while the softer sections remain

within minimum spreads. The following chart (Fig. W-7) has been devised in accordance with a progressive *crescendo* and *diminuendo* for the
purpose of illustrating the various chord extensions with their preferred
spacings, doublings, and fillers. Chords in brackets suggest alternate
spacings with fewer tones.

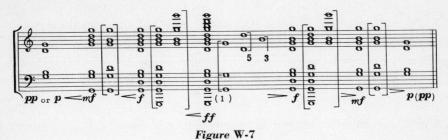

Figure **W-7**

IX. VOICE LEADING

Good voice leading, a trademark of sound craftsmanship, is nowhere
more apparent than in the scoring for wood-wind instruments. Their col-
lective heterogeneous character emphasizes the progression of each voice
line incomparable to the other sections.

Piano music which has inconsistent arrangements of chordal progressions frequently appears as the basis for confusion in this category. These
progressions often have changing registers and varying numbers of chord
tones resulting from purely pianistic considerations. In these instances
the orchestrator should rearrange these elements in more natural, uniform progressions, with smooth, horizontal voice leading.

X. OBBLIGATO OR ADDED SECONDARY PARTS ARRANGED FROM HARMONIC PROGRESSIONS

This classification is perhaps less applicable to the wood-winds than
to the strings or full orchestra. Short secondary counterpoints are effective occasionally if included in fairly large tonal spreads. They should,
of course, be scored with less tonal weight than a principal melody.

XI. ANTIPHONAL EFFECTS

Examples W-30a and b illustrate antiphony with contrasting wood-
wind timbres. Antiphonal overlapping of thematic ideas has some value
in creating continuity and for bridging over rhythmic interest at normal
phrase endings. The method of applying them remains the same as given
for Example S-50.

XII. TREMOLO TYPES

All tremolo types for wood-winds should be regarded as being in the category of special effects and not as regular adjuncts of practical orchestration. They do, however, have some value in dealing with certain aspects of scoring for full orchestra and are analyzed from this point of departure.

The most practical tremolo type for the basic wood-winds (flute, oboe, clarinet, and bassoon) is an extension of the trill approximating the unmeasured, fingered string tremolo and uses the same style of notation. In this form, the size of intervals varies with each player and instrument. Flutes and single reeds are practicable for intervals up to a perfect fifth, while double reeds do not exceed a major third. Inadequacies of intonation and technical difficulties are in proportion to the size of the intervals employed.

Example W-43a

A rather bizarre form of tremolo known as flutter tonguing (Ger. *Flatterzunge*) has been used by some composers since the late 1800s. It has the same notation as that given for the unmeasured, bowed tremolo for strings. This playing style is produced by modifications of double and triple tonguing and is somewhat less successful with double reeds.[1] The sound produced has a variable pitch and harsh tone which belong in the realm of grotesque and fantastic music.

Example W-43b

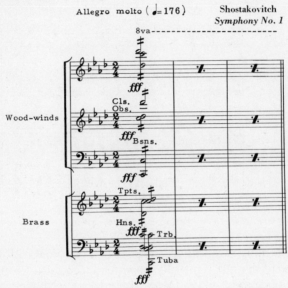

By permission of Leeds Music Corp., New York City.

---

[1] True double and triple tonguing are possible only on the flute, the piccolo, and the brass instruments. Players of the reeds can only approximate the *effect* of these styles through the application of the single-tonguing technique.

Example W-43c

The two examples above need to be examined closely, for the Shosta-kovitch excerpt cannot rightfully be considered flutter tonguing as the sixteenth notes can be played accurately by experienced players using double tonguing. The trumpet parts in Ex. W-43c have the correct nota-tion for this effect as do the wind parts in Ex. I-21.

XIII. DANCE FORMS

Previous structural deductions given for the string section may be applied literally to wood-wind arrangements. Best results with afterbeats will be obtained with a consistent number of interval or chord tones and by keeping them in contrasting timbres with the melodic line. Interlocking is not necessary or desirable here. The following examples are given so that direct comparisons may be made with the settings for strings.

Example W-44

The oboe melody will be in contrast to the afterbeats in the second flute and clarinets. The first flute entrance in the third measure embellishes the cadence.

Example W-45

Albeniz
Sous le palmier, Op. 232, No. 3

The tied-over B's in the first three measures give maximum *sostenuto*. The broken chords, played as intervals by the clarinets, complete the harmonization with the bassoons. Intervals of this kind are particularly effective when played by wood-wind instruments.

Example W-46

Example W-46a has the melody arranged as a dialogue between the melody instruments. The waltz rhythm in the second clarinet and bassoons balances these treble parts. In Example W-46b, the sustained, descending tenor part in the bassoon balances the melody and rhythm instruments. Note the continued oboe parts when the melody is taken over by the flute.

Example W-47

Timbre interplay for the melodic lines is the objective here. The increased tonal spread in the last measures sets up the cadence. Notice the interchange of the repeated interval which permits the same phrasing as for the melody.

Chapter 17

THE BRASS SECTION

Standardization of the brass section for the symphonic orchestra has been a gradual development over a period of several centuries. The final result is a somewhat flexible listing of horns, trumpets, trombones, and tuba, with occasional cornets. Composers still reserve the privilege of determining the number of brass instruments according to their specific needs.

Instrument Standardization
Generalized Analysis of
Sound Production
Chart of Ranges, Clefs, and
Transpositions
Common Characteristics and
Special Effects

The section is not a completely homogeneous grouping, as these instruments vary in construction and means of tone production. For practical purposes, two main divisions within the section can be noted. The horns form a complete unit and are superb in their blending potentials with both the strings and the wood-winds. The trumpets, trombones, and tuba may be classified together as a second unit and are somewhat less adaptable in their blending potentials. As cornets are not regular members of the section, they should be regarded as supplementary instruments. These divisions are the result of differences in construction affecting the bore or tube shape, and of variations in the size and shape of the mouthpiece for each instrument.

The method of tone production is, no doubt, familiar to most students of music. The player's lips, held against various types of cup-shaped mouthpieces, function as vibrating reeds. As the player forces an air stream through the lips, the air column within the tube is set in motion. Various kinds of articulation are brought about by controlled movements of the player's tongue. Thus, the brass player's technique includes a well-regulated coordination of these two human factors. The player's embouchure (position of the lips against the mouthpiece), plus the variants of tonguing (single, double, and triple), combine not only as the means of

THE BRASS INSTRUMENTS

Figure **B-1**

1. All quarter notes indicating range extremes are possible but hazardous for inexperienced players.

2. The best tones are those indicated by whole notes.

3. All range divisions are comparative, being subject to the technical capacities of each performing group.

tone production but also in determining pitch and quality. These technicalities account for the negative as well as the positive aspects of brass playing. They help to explain why some players "crack" on extreme high notes, why very low tones are sometimes "fuzzy," and why attacks are either strong and clear or weak and insecure.

Horns and trumpets with valves and pistons did not become "acceptable" until the middle of the nineteenth century. Before this time composers relied on the old-fashioned "crooked" instruments, with their changing fundamentals and natural series of overtones. Small U-shaped tubings called "crooks," with varying lengths, were inserted in these instruments to change their fundamentals which, in turn, gave forth a well-defined series of overtones. However, all of the tones in these series were not accurate in pitch, nor did they include complete diatonic or chromatic scales. Scale tones not included in a particular series were playable for the horns as *stopped* notes, the hand of the player being inserted in the bell of the instrument to modify the pitch. The trumpets had no such pitch-modifying possibilities and were therefore limited to a half-dozen tones with each change of crooks. Trombones (slide) have always been free from this kind of scale limitation, as changes of fundamentals are arranged by means of altered slide positions. Cornets and tubas, being late nineteenth-century additions to the section, were equipped with pistons which permitted full chromatic scales from the outset. Figure B-1 lists the orchestral brass instruments as they are now constituted.

COMMON CHARACTERISTICS AND SPECIAL EFFECTS

As brass instruments have many common characteristics and technical peculiarities, they can be considered as a unit for certain aspects of tone production.

1. Repeated Notes. Notes in this category employ differing forms of tonguing and are practical at all dynamic levels. Some intonation insecurity and lack of incisiveness is possible in range extremes.

2. Trills. Although trills of minor and major seconds are playable, except for a few note combinations, their effectiveness varies with each instrument and player. Trombone trills are made by means of lip slurs while the other brasses use fingered combinations of valves and pistons. Brass trills are at best somewhat sluggish, blurry, boisterous, and generally lacking in clear intonation. They are of comparatively little value in the normal gamut of practical orchestration.

3. Glissandos. Horns and trombone *glissandos* are possible through the use of a lip slur, providing all of the notes are contained in a single series of overtones. *Glissando* effects, as used by jazz trumpeters, give only a starting note along with a short line indicating the direction of the slide and the word, *rip*. Horn *glissandos* have a boisterous, sweeping effect without being unmusical. When used with trombones, *glissandos* frequently sound vulgar and out of character.

4. Tonguing. All variations of tonguing—single, double, and triple—are essential parts of a brass player's technique. Single tongue strokes are used for all non-*legato* passages and accents, with double and triple tonguing employed for groupings with rapid, multiple-note repetitions. Flutter tonguing is a tremolo type which uses the same notation as that given for the unmeasured, bowed tremolo. It is a special effect reserved for highly evocative passages where a rather ugly sound seems appropriate (see Example I-21).

5. Phrasing. Phrase markings for brass instruments follow the same general patterns as those advised for the wood-winds. All note combinations *without slurs* are played with separate tongue attacks for each note. Short slurs are preferable to long ones, although both forms have been used by composers, markedly so since the trend toward greater melodic importance for the brasses became established in the middle 1800s. Long slurs are found most frequently in solo passages for horns and trombones where a genuine *cantabile* is required. Phrasing is one phase of orchestration which provides the means of tonal articulation and inflection.

6. Breath Control. Proper breath control is a major factor in tone production for all brass instruments. Some idea of the relative importance of this problem may be realized from the fact that the air column in a horn travels some 9 to 18 feet while that for an oboe or clarinet is only slightly more than 2 feet. From this comparison it is obvious that the orchestrator must constantly be aware of this breath factor, especially for the heavier brass instruments. Suitable breaks for changes of breath should be provided and arranged so that they will not interrupt the natural flow of the parts nor disrupt their rhythmic significance.

7. Tonal Strengths. The variation of tonal strengths in the brass section is enormous, covering a dynamic range from an organ-like *pianissimo* to an ear-shattering *fortissimo*. No other section of the orchestra, with the possible exception of the percussion, is so capable of making quick changes in dynamics heard and felt. Separately and collectively, the brass instruments have the strongest tonal strengths and weights in the orchestra —a constant factor in estimating the details of tonal balance. The everpresent danger of over-scoring for the section is one which the orchestrator must constantly evaluate within an orchestral perspective. There are limitations beyond which combined string and wood-wind sonorities become submerged by the tonal strength of the brass. The task is to unite these elements with good blendings for tonal balance based on the recognition of the comparative tonal strengths of each section.

8. Mutes. Theoretically, all brass parts can be muted.

Actually, mutes are not always available for horns and tubas, especially in most secondary orchestras. This fact should not be overlooked, since a single unmuted part, playing with a muted section, conspicuously alters the whole tonal effect. Mutes not only reduce volume; they also change tone quality. With them there is a tendency toward faulty intonation, especially with inexperienced players of horns and trombones. Although muted brass is capable of playing the softest possible dynamics, it can cut through string and wood-wind *tuttis* with little difficulty. Muted brass, now a commonplace effect, has musical value in indirect proportion to the frequency of its use.

9. Signatures. Limited scale tones for the natural horns and trumpets undoubtedly led to the practice of omitting key signatures for these instruments. All parts for them were written in C and accidentals added as needed. After valves and pistons were introduced, some theorists urged the abolition of the older form of notation in favor of using signatures for all the brass instruments and timpani. Yet it still remains an unsettled question as orchestrators continue to follow their own preferences.

Brass instrument players unfamiliar with key signatures are apt to overlook them, and, by playing in the wrong key, may inflict unintentional discords on the listener. However, if all brass and timpani parts were to be consistently written with signatures, the practice would soon alter the present confusion which has been inherited from more than two centuries of notation designed for instruments that are now obsolete. These remarks do not apply to cornets, trombones, and tubas, as they were never affected by the older notation practices.

Chapter 18

THE HORNS

(Fr. *cor;* It. *corno;* Ger. *Horn*)

A brief survey of notation problems peculiar to the natural horns is indispensable for intelligible score reading. These are problems directly attributable to a system of notation based on the necessity for changing fundamentals. The original valveless horn as developed for the orchestra came from its earlier prototype, the hunting horn. (The military bugle is a surviving type of natural horn that is still in common use.) Crooks of differing lengths were used, more or less frequently during the course of a composition, to raise or lower the instrument's fundamental compatible with changing key tonalities. Disadvantages of this impractical system, not superficially discernible, included many inadequacies of tone production. The good tones (open) had to be matched with the poorer ones (stopped) which were not accurate in pitch. Furthermore, fundamentals and four notes in each harmonic series were of such poor quality as to make them generally impracticable. Scale limitations for a horn in C may be better understood from the notation given in Fig. B-2.

Natural Horns
Crooks
Changing Fundamentals
Harmonic Series
Transpositions
Notation
Valve Horn in F
Playing Characteristics

THE HARMONIC SERIES

| 1 | 2 | 3 | 4 | 5 | 6 | 7 | 8 | 9 | 10 | 11 | 12 | 13 | 14 | 15 | 16 |

Figure B-2

In this series, the fundamental C, along with notes numbered 7, 11, 13, and 14 were impracticable. Composers using this fundamental not only had an incomplete C major scale but very few tones that would fit with simple harmonic modulations. Until well after 1850, attempts were made to circumvent this difficulty by either frequent crook changes and/or by writing horns in pairs with different fundamentals. The purpose of this expedient was to have horns with two or more harmonic series available, from which a maximum of good tones could be extracted for a principal key and simple modulations. This system was the accepted method for natural horns (and trumpets) until the final decades of the nineteenth century.

The end result of this practice was that composers were restricted to keeping melodic lines to a single instrument and were forced to write horn parts which alternated between those with dissimilar fundamentals. The incompleteness of scales accounts for the unexpected voids found in the melodic lines in the horn parts of many Classic scores. The following chart lists the most common horn fundamentals with their respective transpositions.

HORN PITCHES AND TRANSPOSITIONS

Figure **B-3**

The notation of this chart illustrates the system of writing all parts in C, the crook length in each instance automatically establishing the pitch and degree of transposition. Written notes thus become signs for playing positions rather than signs for actual pitch, a practice common to all transposing instruments. The interval of transposition is determined by the interval degree of difference between C and the pitch designation, which is always placed *below* C, as given. Treble-clef parts for transposing instruments are written *higher* than they sound, with few exceptions.

However, this method of transposition is reversed for horn parts using the bass clef. The confusing custom of inverting the interval of transposition for bass-clef parts sets the notation an octave too low. In the twentieth century, orchestrators usually use the same intervals of transposition for treble and bass clefs. In such cases it is advisable to add a note of explanation on the system used for all horn parts requiring the bass clef. Example B-1 illustrates both types of notation.

Example B-1

The practical expedient of writing for natural horns with differing fundamentals is well illustrated in the following Weber excerpt. The harmonic progressions here never stray from the principal C major triads, yet the composer needed the horns in F and C so that a maximum of open tones would be available for this style of quartet writing, which was something of an innovation in its day.

Example B-2

The full implications for the choice of these two fundamentals may be better evaluated after combining the two harmonic series as given in Fig. B-4.

THE HARMONIC SERIES IN C AND F

Figure **B-4**

From this multitude of natural horns, the valve horn in F has emerged as the generally accepted, sole survivor for orchestral scoring. Valve combinations change the fundamental of this instrument, thereby producing a full chromatic scale throughout its entire compass. It now serves as an all-purpose, "all-in-one" instrument. Its universal adoption does, however, require the player to make the transpositions from the older notations, along with those parts written in C by a few twentieth-century composers.

The horn in F has the advantage of being a middle-range instrument which places its best-playing two-octave spread where it is most needed. Its highest "insecure" tones are made more playable by the use of a double horn in F and B♭ with a fourth valve. With this extra valve, these top notes become less difficult even for the inexperienced player.

PLAYING CHARACTERISTICS OF THE HORN IN F

The extraordinary blending qualities of the horn, its eloquent power as a solo instrument, plus its usefulness in adding strength and substance to the strings and wood-winds, distinguish it as the most valued member of the brass section. Its middle two octaves have an evenness of tone which is ideal either alone or in combination with other instruments. The lowest augmented fourth, starting on F, is noticeably weaker in carrying power than the middle or higher ranges, and this tonal difference prevails in loud passages regardless of the amount of unison doubling. This characteristic is not so serious a handicap in exposed solo passages in moderately soft dynamics. The highest sixth of its range demands a firm, sure embouchure and good breath control, which combine to make it a precarious range for the average player, especially if a double horn is not used. These highest tones are particularly difficult to control in the softer dynamic levels.

The horn is a peerless solo instrument capable of great expressiveness. Although its best results are obtained in comparatively slow tempos, the more rapid passages sound surprisingly clear and vital. Horn tone is distinguishable from the other brass instruments in that it is rounder, mellower, and slightly less precise in its attacks. Accents are less sharp and biting than those of trumpets and trombones. There is strength and weight, without coarseness. Some representative solo passages which illustrate its versatility are given in Example B-3.

Example B-3

HORNS

The horns are unexcelled in adding depth and substance to melodic lines and figurations in the strings and/or wood-winds. This applies to doublings with the horn either in unison or octaves and is particularly rewarding in the softer dynamics where there may be multiple-voice accompaniments. It is a scoring combination to be found quite frequently in the works of the Romantic composers.

Example B-4

Other forms of doubling include outlining (Example B-5a) and chord repetitions derived from melodic figurations (Example B-5b). Both types have tonal depth without distortion of the principal melodic ideas.

Example B-5

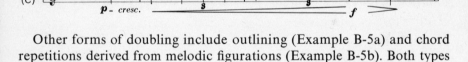

Example B-5 *(continued)*

By permission of Boosey-Hawkes, Inc., New York and London.

Horns have a second method of producing stopped, or muted, tones in addition to that made with a mute. It is achieved by combining lip tension and overblowing with the hand inserted far into the bell. Notation for this effect has crosses (+) over each note, usually with the word "brassy" or "*cuivré*" and a circle (○) over the note which starts the resumption of normal playing. The tone quality of notes thus stopped has a nasal, metallic twang in the stronger dynamics and a thin, distant sound at the softer levels. When used for accents, the attack is sharp and biting. The following example illustrates the markings for both types of stopped tone.

Example B-6

Reprint by permission of Jean Jobert, Paris, Copyright owner, Elkan-Vogel Co., Inc., Philadelphia, Pa., agents.

Copyright for all countries, J. and W. Chester Ltd., London.

No other instrument has the same capacity for binding harmonic elements together with such sure results. A single note, sustained from a harmonic progression, can often create greater coherence and continuity than whole chords sustained in other sections. This unique feature of the horn has been fully exploited by composers of all periods.

Example B-7

By permission of Boosey-Hawkes, Inc., New York and London.

Parts for *natural* horns are in three general categories: (1) short melodic phrases rather than full-length melodies, (2) limited sustaining elements, and (3) semifanfare figurations developed from the principal triads usually for cadences. In category 3, trumpets and timpani were invariably combined with the horns. Notation was necessarily *diatonic* and became a somewhat stereotyped formula.

Example B-8

The advent of the valve horn tended to reduce this kind of stylized writing and to replace it with newer characteristic passages of strong, bold melodic ideas. A new perspective of melodic strength thus became part of a movement toward greater emphasis of the brass section.

Example B-9

By permission of C. F. Peters Corporation, 373 Fourth Ave., New York, N.Y.

By permission of C. F. Peters Corporation, 373 Fourth Ave., New York, N.Y.

Horns are very effective in proclaiming principal thematic ideas, either alone or in combination with other brass instruments. This distinctive feature has been well established in the opening measures of many symphonic movements.

Example B-10

Although horns blend well with strings and wood-winds, there is a marked difference in tone quality when they are paired with trumpets. The latter's sharper, crisper attack and brighter tone tends to give a two-dimensional sound effect which can be disturbing under certain conditions. Yet there are times when no other combination will suffice. Some unequal tonal weights resulting from combined horns and trumpets may be compensated for by the overlapping of parts on intervals and chords. This tonal discrepancy is not serious for horns paired with trombones, as their tone qualities are more similar.

Figure **B-5a**

Figure **B-5b**

The setting in Fig. B-5b illustrates the desirability of considering strong and weak tonal strengths for chord progressions to be played by unequal timbres because the voice leading will be conspicuous. When this kind of passage occurs, it is often best to select good-sounding intervals for the strongest timbres, filling out the chords with the weaker strengths. Furthermore, it will be useful to remember that dissonant intervals have less potency when played by light timbres than when overshadowed by heavier tonal strengths.

Chapter 19

THE HORNS AS
AN INDEPENDENT CHOIR

Notation
Four-part Writing
Spacings

Although scoring for one horn is not unprecedented, horns in pairs are preferable for orchestras, even with a minimum instrumentation. The practice of using horns in pairs, dating back to the earliest Classical scores, led to a practical, unique expedient not common with the other wind instruments. This developed the need for specialization of playing in either high or low registers. Accordingly, horn players have justifiably concentrated on developing an embouchure adaptable to either medium-to-high or medium-to-low range spreads. This operating practice has resulted in horns being interlocked and written as follows: high, I–III; low, II–IV. The voice parts for four horns are therefore not written in the numerical order as they appear on the score page. These changes in voice allocations are shown in Fig. B-6.

Figure B-6

Four horns in their normal playing range have the same tonal spread as a male chorus plus an extra higher fourth for the first horn. Four-part harmonizations for the male chorus frequently require a shifting of the melodic line to inside parts because of range limitations. A similar situation exists in many settings of four-part chorals for the horn quartet. In scoring *America* in its usual key (G) for these instruments, it will be observed that although the melody of the first six measures fits the range of the first horn, the high *tessitura* of the last eight measures makes literal transcription impossible. Compensating adjustments are: (1) inverting the melody an octave lower which places the alto part *above* the melody, (2) lowering the melody an octave but keeping the harmony parts *below* it. A reduction in the number of voice parts is frequently desirable when arranging the melody as the highest part. These alternative arrangements are shown in the following settings.

Example B-11

Melodies written as inside parts will be more audible if the harmony parts have a minimum of movement (Example B-11b). These settings emphasize the relative importance of complete melody tessituras in all scoring plans. They further demonstrate the position of key tonalities in respect to the total tonal spread of the parts. *America,* transposed either to the key of D or E♭, would permit the original four-part arrangement to be set quite literally.

A pair of horns in small-orchestra combinations is the greatest single source of brilliance and tonal strength. When combined with a bassoon, it constitutes a reasonably even timbred sonority for three-voice chord progressions. Complete dynamic flexibility in the middle register makes the horns invaluable, either alone or in combination. Full-chord writing is, however, less frequent for the smaller ensembles than for full-orchestra instrumentation. Scoring four horns for a large orchestra is an extension of the idiomatic uses carried out for the smaller groups. The differences that will occur are those dealing chiefly with larger tonal extensions, expanded chordal spacings, and greater breadth in the statement of melodic and rhythmic ideas.

Chord writing for a horn quartet is generally clearer if confined to three-voice progressions. In this voice pattern, the highest or lowest notes are sometimes doubled in unison, depending upon the desired point of extra strength. In the softer dynamics this unison doubling is unnecessary. Chord progressions sound smoothest when there is a minimum of movement to nearest tones.

The student orchestrator is advised to study horn parts in their full context in the scores listed below. Since voice textures vary in accordance with the structural dimensions and musical scope of each work, idiomatic values can be better appraised by examining these parts for both small and large instrumentations.

SMALL ORCHESTRA

Mozart, Symphony No. 35
Beethoven, Symphony No. 8
Wagner, Richard, *Siegfried Idyll*
Debussy, *L'Après-midi d'un faune*
Falla, *El Amor Brujo*
Prokofiev, *Classical Symphony*

LARGE ORCHESTRA

Beethoven, Symphony No. 9
Brahms, *Academic Festival Overture*
Tchaikovsky, Symphony No. 4
Hindemith, *Mathis der Maler*
Bartók, Concerto for Orchestra
Williams, R. Vaughan, Symphony in F minor

Chapter 20

THE TRUMPET

(Fr. *trompette;* It. *tromba;* Ger. *Trompete*)

The evolution of the trumpet as an orchestral instrument parallels that of the horn. Original trumpet models were valveless, resembling somewhat the military bugle. The tone was brilliant and powerful but scalewise, inflexible. A comparison of natural trumpets and horns crooked in C will clarify their basic similarities. With this fundamental, the trumpet would be approximately half the tube length of the horn. Accordingly, the trumpet's best tones sound an octave higher than those of the horn, harmonics 3 to 12 in the series: ten tones in all. Some modifications of these basic tones were made for semitones through the use of varying lip pressures.

HARMONIC SERIES FOR TRUMPET IN C

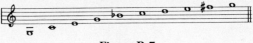

Figure **B-7**

Trumpet parts intended for music other than that in C required crook changes with fundamentals agreeing with each new key tonality. The fol-

218

lowing chart lists these pitches, their transpositions, and their range placements. Attention is directed toward the first four pitches: F, E, E♭, and D. Parts for these crookings *invert* the normal interval of transposition and are written *lower* than they sound.

TRUMPET PITCHES, TRANSPOSITIONS, RANGE PLACEMENTS

Figure B-8

The practical values to be derived from an understanding of the methods used for valveless trumpets (and horns) are twofold. First, they account for the many irregularities of interval, chord, and melodic writing found in numberless Classic and early Romantic scores. Secondly, the modern trumpet has evolved from its earlier prototype as an "all-in-one" instrument with valve combinations automatically giving a complete cycle of fundamentals in a chromatic sequence.

ORCHESTRAL PARTS FOR NATURAL TRUMPETS

The rather florid trumpet parts with unusually high *tessituras* occurring in the scores of the Baroque period are not to be construed as carrying over beyond the works of Johann Sebastian Bach. This style of playing, known as *clarion,* became, for all practical purposes, a lost art with the advent of the more homophonic style of composition developed by the post-Bach composers. Accordingly, trumpet parts became less melodic and more functional as harmonic supports, in keeping with the structural changes.

Orchestral parts for the natural trumpet are, in the main, quite similar to those for the natural horn. Their rather stereotyped functions include: (1) long sustained notes at all dynamic levels, (2) quasi-fanfare figurations, (3) brief statements of principal thematic ideas for emphasis, (4) chord outlining mostly of major triads, (5) building cadential climaxes with their stronger tonal weights, and (6) emphasis of isolated melodic notes and/or accented chord tones. Extended phrases of *cantabile* are conspicuously absent. Excerpts in Example B-12 illustrate, in part, typical trumpet passages in these categories. (Review Examples B-8a and b for (4) and (5).)

Example B-12

Some idea of the melodic voids imposed on the composer by the technical limitations of the natural trumpet may be realized from the parts for it in the overture to *Fidelio* by Beethoven. In this overture the composer used exactly three different notes in octaves I, IV, and V! The important detail here is to observe the *ways* in which these three notes were used. Other scores of the period are equally revealing in this respect, and much basic knowledge can be gained by study concentrated on the combined horn, trumpet, and timpani parts, as they constituted the sole source of tonal brilliance for orchestral music of that time.

In a study of natural horn and trumpet parts, one perplexing detail of notation may be noted. Frequently, logical interval sequences are disrupted by seemingly needless unison doublings. It appears that Classic composers resorted to these doublings as an expedient for maintaining maximum brass sonorities, at the expense of a loss in orchestral balance. These interval dislocations, resulting from scale voids, should not be considered as valid models. A detailed analysis of this problem and suggested corrections are given in Felix Weingartner's book *On the Performance of Beethoven's Symphonies.* The following trumpet excerpts illustrate unfortunate scale difficulties connected with the use of natural trumpets.

Example B-13

THE VALVE TRUMPET

The gradual acceptance of a trumpet with valves paved the way for a new approach to its potentialities both as a solo and ensemble instrument. With scale restrictions removed, its new flexibility and responsiveness could be applied to melodic ideas and figurations heretofore possible only in the wood-winds. Symphonic scores after 1850 show the composers' awareness of its capacities for *cantabile* and extraordinary agility with figurations having large and unusual intervals. Trumpet parts became more important melodically, more active rhythmically, and more conspicuous dynamically for peak accents and climaxes. A comparison of the excerpts given in Example B-14 with those previously shown for natural trumpets reveals the extent to which changes occurred.

Example B-14

Example B-14 *(continued)*

With permission of the Verlag F.E.C. Leukart, Munich-Leipzig.

Copyright 1955 by G. Schirmer, Inc., New York, N.Y. Used by permission of the copyright owner.

The superior tonal strength of the trumpet is an important consideration, as it is the highest voice part in the brass section. Its brilliant, piercing tone can cut through any orchestral fabric, yet its softer tones are rewardingly smooth and well voiced for subdued melodic ideas. It responds finely to all tonguing styles and trills. There are no serious tonal breaks in its compass other than some comparatively minor insecurities with the lowest tones. However, extremes of range, both high and low, are difficult to control in the softer dynamic levels.

Fortissimo in muted trumpets, in the medium-to-high range, has brilliant, but brassy, carrying power. When played *pianissimo,* muted trumpets in two or three parts produce an effect which all but defies description; they become phantom trumpets of another sphere. Debussy caught this color well in the second of his orchestral *Nocturnes, Fêtes.*

Example B-15

Reprint by permission of Jean Jobert, Paris, Copyright owner, Elkan-Vogel Co., Inc., Philadelphia, Pa., agents.

The basic playing formulas developed for the natural trumpet have been retained for the valve instrument. Composers have simply developed their range and scope in keeping with the newer and broader concepts of orchestral thinking. Their creative expansiveness with orchestral textures has resulted in increased technical skill on the part of players.

It is the ever-present danger of *overwriting* for the trumpets which should be watched. The trumpet and its music need constant reevaluation in the perspective of context, appropriateness, and musical value. It should not be used indiscriminately for artificial doublings or for effects far removed from the music it seeks to enhance.

The trumpet in F, the one most commonly found in symphonic scores dating from the 1850s, has been supplanted by ones in C and B♭. The trumpet in C appears to have been favored by European composers, possibly because of practical reasons of notation as recommended by Richard Strauss in his revision of the *Treatise on Instrumentation* by Hector Berlioz. The theory set forth by Strauss is that written parts in C would facilitate and standardize notation inasmuch as trumpet parts are not always played by the instrument that is designated. This theory has been accepted in principle and, to some extent, has been practiced by American composers and trumpeters of major symphony orchestras.

However, the trumpet in B♭ is the choice of the great majority of players and is the one to write for. This instrument has the advantage of an extra slide, or spiral-key mechanism, which changes its B♭ fundamental to that of A, thereby making it serviceable for all key tonalities. A choice between the two is determined, as with the clarinets, by the key deviations from C major, B♭ being used for flat keys and A for those with sharps. The use of key signatures is recommended.

Chapter 21

THE CORNET

(Fr. *piston, cornet à pistons;* It. *cornetts;* Ger. *Kornett*)

	Tonal Qualities
	Playing Characteristics

Some confusion exists concerning the tonal differences between the trumpet and the cornet. Since the 1920s, trumpet-model cornets have been introduced, thereby increasing this confusion. Most symphony conductors would not agree with some theorists that tonal differences between the two instruments are slight and inconsequential. The fact remains that the cornet's tube length and shape are not the same as those of the trumpet and neither are the size and shape of its mouthpiece. These differences account for a distinctive set of tonal values for each instrument. The cornet has a round, mellow, smooth tone, but with less brilliance and power than the trumpet. It excels in flexibility, agility, and lyric expressiveness—qualities which distinguish it as the best high-range brass instrument for *cantabile* melody and for rapid, intricate passages. Its tonal qualities lie between those of the horn and trumpet and have playing characteristics of each. Representative parts for cornets can be examined in the Symphony in D minor by Franck, the *Capriccio Italien* by Tchaikovsky, and the ballet *Petrouchka* by Stravinsky.

Cornets are not to be considered as regular members of the brass section but rather as supplementary, auxiliary instruments. A choice of B♭ or A crooking will be determined in the same manner as that given for the trumpets. They are ordinarily used in pairs, have the same written and sounding ranges as the trumpets, and are given parts spanning the soprano-alto registers.

Chapter 22

THE TROMBONES

(Fr. *trombone;* It. *trombone;* Ger. *Posaune*)

Sound Production
Slide Positions
Clefs

The trombone is a fully developed facsimile of its earlier prototype, the medieval *sackbut*. This "noble" instrument did not become established in symphonic instrumentation until Beethoven's time (Fifth Symphony); yet it was used by opera composers dating back to 1565. The true trombone is built with a pair of tubular slides which distinguish it from all other wind instruments, since it is the only one capable of making its own pitch, as does the human voice. Variations of pitch are regulated by the position of the slide, which alters the length of the air column within the tube. Valve trombones, although used in some European orchestras and bands, have not met universal acceptance.

THE TENOR TROMBONE

The tenor trombone in B♭ is the one universally used and is non-transposing in all clefs except the treble. The technical aspects of the slide positions are unique with wind instruments. Whereas the other brass instruments produce a cycle of changing fundamentals and harmonic series by means of valve combinations, the trombone accomplishes similar changes by means of slide positions. There are seven positions of the slide for the completion of a chromatic-scale cycle. Figure B-9 lists these fundamentals with each harmonic series and their slide positions.

225

TROMBONE (B♭ TENOR) FUNDAMENTALS, HARMONIC SERIES, AND SLIDE POSITIONS

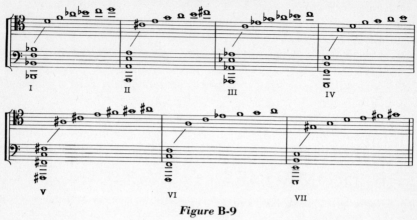

Figure **B-9**

In the first position, the slide is pulled up tight and then extended proportionately for the other six positions. Adjacent positions can be played almost instantaneously; others, farther apart, require split seconds for their execution. Rapid passages containing awkward slide positions (Fig. B-10) should be avoided since they are not playable with any degree of clarity, style, or good intonation.

Figure **B-10**

Composers since the time of Gluck have, with few exceptions, consistently written for three trombones as a unit of "harmony instruments." This arrangement has the advantage of spanning the two middle and bottom parts. Up to the twentieth century, these parts were written in the alto, tenor, and bass clefs. With the increased acceptance of the valve trumpet, the alto trombone was gradually discarded in favor of either three tenors or two tenors and a bass. This change removed the necessity for further use of the alto clef, the tenor and bass being adequate for the notation of newer groupings. (**Note:** The treble clef, as used in some orchestrations of music for school orchestras, is an expedient to facilitate notation for players not familiar with the bass clef; it is not recommended here.)

THE BASS TROMBONE

The bass trombone pitched in F is a perfect fourth lower than the tenor instrument. Its first position has the identical fundamental and harmonic series as that given for the sixth position of the tenor trombone. The bass instrument has about three more feet of tubing than its smaller counterpart, which necessitates the need for increased breath and embouchure control. A separate F attachment is used occasionally to convert the tenor trombone to the equal playing potentials of the larger instrument with identical slide positions.

All tonguing styles are possible, but the more rapid ones are fatiguing and become sluggish, especially in the lowest register. The deep, full tone of the bass trombone makes it ideally suited to the bass parts of all brass ensemble passages. It is rarely used as a solo instrument unless doubled either in unison or octaves. Extremely rapid notations are less satisfactory than those for the lighter tenor instrument.

Chapter 23

THE TROMBONES AS A UNIT

Group Instruments
Playing Characteristics
Harmony Playing

Hector Berlioz, in his monumental *Treatise on Instrumentation,* referred to the trombones as "group instruments." This distinction results from their homogeneous tonal qualities, which vary little throughout their ranges. Any variance which may occur is generally the fault of the player's execution of range extremes.

In the Richard Strauss revision of the Berlioz text, isolated examples are given as evidence questioning the Berlioz premise. In certain contexts the Strauss theory, supporting independent part writing, may have some validity, but it is too specific to be taken generally. The Berlioz observation, made a century ago, to the effect that "a single trombone in an orchestra seems more or less out of place," remains equally valid today as when it was written.

The single trombone parts in the Chopin piano concertos are glaring examples of ineffectual writing. Many passages sound inappropriate, weak, and slightly amateurish. These parts are rarely idiomatic and frequently give the impression of being intended for a kind of brass bassoon. Trombone doubling of adequately scored bass parts and added extraneous harmonic fillers do not increase volume; rather they upset a normal balanced sonority.

The basic weakness of these parts lies in the composer's failure to recognize the trombone's natural affinity for harmony playing. This particular reference is of value in appraising commercial orchestrations designed primarily for theater, school, and amateur ensembles. With these, parts for one trombone are essentially utilitarian, being a combination of doubled bass parts, cues from other instruments, and occasional chord tones and melodic lines. The results are, for the most part, functional rather than artistic. If one trombone is to be included in varying instrumentations, it can approach artistic standards if employed idiomatically with the other brass instruments.

At this point the student orchestrator may acquire an expanded perspective through a study of the parts for two trombones in Beethoven's Sixth Symphony, the *Pastoral*. A comparison with that of the Chopin concertos reveals the extent of differences in approach and understanding between the two composers. The Beethoven score clearly indicates the advantages to be derived from using trombones as "group instruments" for harmony playing. Part writing for three trombones is similarly exploited by Beethoven in his Fifth and Ninth Symphonies.

Orchestrators writing for three trombones should be cognizant of difficulties arising from the possible absence of a bass instrument. It is rarely available for most orchestras other than those of major standing, and its absence can cause considerable distortion to harmonic positions. Low-part writing, designed for a bass trombone, must invariably be played an *octave higher* if assigned to a third tenor instrument, which automatically alters chord positions. Figure B-11 illustrates the distortions resulting from these inverted parts.

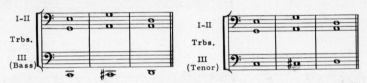

Figure **B-11**

Trombones are particularly well adapted to harmony playing in all categories of homophonic music. Their extra tonal weight as a unit makes them indispensable for increasing the solidity of harmonic factors. The group-harmony method of scoring has been consistently recognized by symphonic composers dating back to the early Classic period. Later composers have enlarged the scope of this method but they have not strayed far from its basic formulas.

Example B-16

Example B-16 *(continued)*

Copyright 1934 by B. Schott's Soehne, Mainz; by permission of Associated Music Publishers, Inc.

In polyphonic music, the trombone's playing potentials are somewhat more limited. They are best reserved for outlining canonic entrances, for emphasis of isolated accented notes, and for occasional statement of principal thematic ideas in peak climaxes. Notation for outlining can usually be derived from the first notes of rapid scale passages, thereby giving harmonic definition. Melodic statement is most successful when confined to notations which allow clear articulation.

Example B-17

Schumann
Symphony No. 4

Part writing in the softer dynamic levels is particularly felicitous, approximating the sonority of a male chorus.

Example B-18

The long *legato* slurs indicated in these excerpts are rather exceptional and differ in style from those employed by the other brass instruments. The only true trombone *legato* is made by a lip slur confined to the note in each harmonic series. These lip slurs can be made only in the upper register. All other *legato* phrasings are the result of lip slurs combined with changing slide positions. This technique produces a *portamento* style of *legato* which is best in moderate tempos.

Unslurred *cantabile* melodies are played by tonguing each note. These tones can be nicely connected in a characteristic style approaching *legato,* which is applicable to all dynamics. At the softer levels the tone is solid without harshness, while unisons in the tenor range with louder dynamics are penetratingly virile.

Example B-19

Example B-19 *(continued)*

This semidetached style of melody playing, in unisons or octaves, has its peak strength in the middle and upper reaches of the tenor range. The characteristic pungency of parts in this register is sacrificed if doubled by other instruments.

Example B-20

Solo undoubled melody passages of any significant length for the trombone are comparatively rare. This void is particularly noticeable with sustained *cantabile* melodies of principal thematic interest. The noble tone quality of the instrument is well realized in Example B-21. Other solos of similar character occur in the middle section of the Sibelius Symphony No. 7 and in the *Adagio* movement of the Saint-Saëns Symphony No. 3.

Example B-21

Short thematic solos are, on the other hand, both effective and quite numerous. They have interest and continuity when paired antiphonally with horns or trumpets.

Example B-22

Unison and/or octave passages, with or without doublings in the brass, have assumed an ever-increasing place of importance since the late 1900s. A maximum of sonority, power, and brilliance can be achieved by doubling the trombones in a higher octave with the trumpets. It is a device useful for establishing contrast, melodic emphasis, and tonal weight. Example B-23e illustrates one method of building brass sonority for a *crescendo* with an ascending melodic line.

Example B-23

By permission of C. F. Peters Corp., 373 Fourth Ave., New York, N.Y.

Example B-23 (*continued*)

By permission of Leeds Music Corp., New York.

The third trombone and tuba occasionally have bass parts when the cellos are diverted to melodic passages and figurations in the tenor register. Such parts usually have a minimum of movement and are frequently doubled by the bassoons. Contrabass doubling occurs less often.

Example B-24

By permission of Universal Edition, Vienna and London.

Muted trombones, though commonplace for solo parts or in combination with other instruments, are seldom scored as a three-part *soli* unit. This is rather surprising, as the timbre of this muted ensemble is capable of unusual possibilities along the lines shown for the trumpets in Example B-15. It is the kind of tone quality which responds well to light doublings provided that parts are left well exposed.

Example B-25

By permission of Southern Music Publishing Company, Inc., New York, N.Y.

Chapter 24

THE TUBA
(Fr. *tuba;* It. *tuba;* Ger. *Tuba*)

Most Common Types
Playing Characteristics, Singly
and with Trombones
Tonal Qualities
Idiomatic Uses

The tuba became part of the brass section for large symphonic orchestration during the last decades of the nineteenth century. It supplanted the now obsolete ophicleide as the lowest-pitched brass instrument. In tone quality, mouthpiece, and bore, the tuba may be considered as a super-bass cornet although it embodies some tonal characteristics of the horn and the trumpet. Its position in the brass choir is analogous to the contrabasses in the string section.

Considerable confusion exists concerning the size and pitch of tubas upon which the orchestrator can rely. The possible, but not probable, ones include those in B♭, F, E♭, C, and BB♭. Although a choice of tubas may be practicable for a few players in major symphony orchestras, no such choice exists for the vast majority of players in the secondary orchestras of this country. The reason for limiting a preference for E♭ and BB♭ instruments is both practical and economic.

A large number of players of this cumbersome and expensive instrument are frequently recruited from bands where these tubas are standard. Of the two, the one in E♭ is most frequently available. Sousaphones, with their rearranged bell positions, are strictly band instruments and should not be considered for orchestration. Tubas are equipped with a set of valves or rotary pistons which change fundamentals and harmonic series in much the same manner as for other valve instruments. Although four-valve models with a slightly extended range exist, the three-valve instrument is standard for the great majority of orchestras.

The range difference of a diminished fourth between the E♭ and BB♭ tubas is a major consideration in writing for them. The same words of caution directed toward the writing for three trombones apply equally well to when they are combined with a tuba. The lowest tones of a BB♭ tuba have to be either omitted or inverted if played on an E♭ instrument. If the latter expedient is resorted to, chord positions become dislocated, as indicated in Fig. B-12.

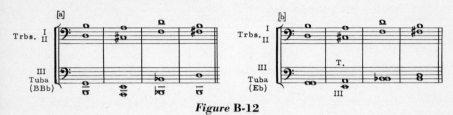

Figure B-12

Tuba playing requires an enormous amount of breath which, to some extent, affects the style of writing for it. Long sustained notes are not advisable, yet extended figurations and scale passages, either *legato* or *staccato,* are fairly common. Tuba tone quality, at its best, is smooth, round, and solid—akin to that of the cornet. It does not have the same crisp, sharp attack of the trumpets or trombones. The instrument is capable of considerable technical agility despite its rather ponderous tones in the lowest octave. Large intervals are no more difficult for the tuba than for the other valve instruments. This asset is used occasionally to vary the *tessitura* of bass parts which might otherwise seem static.

Lyric solo melodies for the tuba are quite uncommon. Although extreme *tessituras* are generally avoided, the following excerpts illustrate two composers' treatment of the medium-to-low and medium-to-high ranges in a most effective manner.

Example B-26

Copyright 1955 by G. Schirmer, Inc., New York, N.Y. Used by permission of the copyright owner.

The low register can be controlled reasonably well at all dynamic levels, but the higher tones with strong dynamics tend to be strident with an all-engulfing tonal power.

Example B-27

Muted tubas are not generally practicable. Although they are standard for major orchestras, the players in most secondary orchestras rarely have mutes available. Few scores call for them and they are cumbersome at best. The orchestrator must be prepared for this eventuality when writing for muted tuba and trombones. Although four-part writing for this combination can be effective as a special coloristic device, an unmuted tuba with muted trombones would resemble the bellow of a giant struggling with the cries of pygmies.

Phrase markings here follow the same general pattern as for the other brass instruments. Bright *staccato* notes are the closest brass approach to the string *pizzicato*. Accented attacks are good if confined to comparatively short sections. All tonguing styles are playable but with some sluggishness to be noted in low registers having rapid articulation.

Example B-28

By permission of Boosey-Hawkes, Inc., New York and London.

Copyright 1935 in U.S.A. and all countries by the Oxford University Press. Reprinted by permission.

Chapter 25

SCORING THE BRASS AS
AN INDEPENDENT SECTION

> *Functional Adaptations*
> *Voice Allocations*
> *Structural Expansions*

Scoring the brass instruments as an independent section takes divergent paths from those previously considered for the strings and wood-winds. The dissimilar approach is due partly to the heterogeneous character of the brass section and partly to the limited scope of the idiomatic playing potentials of each instrument. In addition, the divisions within the section form homogeneous tonal clusters of horns, trumpets, and trombones with tuba. Their separate and combined ranges and tonal strengths determine voice distribution, fillers, and doublings. The whole conception of scoring for the brass section is so radically different from that of the other sections that it necessitates a totally changed set of values, perceptions, and objectives.

The scoring of chorals for the brass in varying numbers provides excellent experience in appraising the many problems occasioned by differing strengths and ranges. Practically identical compasses for horns and trombones, spanning the treble and bass registers, account for some unavoidable overlapping and doubling of parts. This normal playing range is similar to that of a male chorus. The trumpet's total range corresponds to that of a women's chorus solely in the treble clef. The full brass section therefore spans the tonal spread of a mixed chorus which, in turn, necessitates some doubling of inside parts.

The soprano, alto, and tenor parts can, with proper transpositions, be transcribed literally for three trumpets. Part writing will differ somewhat for adaptations for two trumpets (Example B-31).

Example B-29

America

Melody *tessituras* assume the same relative importance for trombones and tuba as found in the horn settings of *America* in Example B-11. Mixed-chorus parts must first be transposed to male-chorus ranges, which involves some close-position chord progressions in the bass clef. These positions, if not too numerous, are not serious enough to obscure clear part writing.

Example B-30a

A second setting with open-position chords has some advantages, especially if used with treble-clef parts as given in Example B-30b. Melodies placed in inside parts tend to be unclear unless there is a minimum of movement in the other parts.

Example B-30b

The second strain of *America* can be set literally by lowering all mixed-chorus parts by an octave.

Scoring chorals for a quartet of mixed brasses (trumpets and horns) necessitates some rearrangement of parts due to unequal tonal strengths, as noted in Example B-15. Occasional overlapping of the alto and tenor parts is both inevitable and desirable in establishing good voice leading for the tonally stronger trumpets. The weaker horns can be adjusted to fit these voice patterns.

Example B-31

The addition of a trombone to the trumpet-horn quartet alters primarily the voice lines of the horns. With this grouping, it is desirable to have the two trumpets and trombone sound well together as a three-part unit and to readjust the inside harmony parts accordingly. With a low-melody *tessitura* some unison doublings will occur, while higher melodic lines allow better spacings.

Example B-32

Scoring *America* for a full brass section places each division in the ranges normally used for full orchestra: (1) The four horns take over the inverted chords, as given in Example I-27d. (2) The three trumpets remain unchanged (Example B-29). (3) The first and second trombones have harmony parts which will sound well with the trumpets and the bass octaves in the third trombone and tuba. The single melodic line in the first trumpet has sufficient tonal strength to carry the part adequately with the other supporting harmony instruments.

Example B-33

Chapter 26

THE BRASS SECTION IN
FULL ORCHESTRAL SCORING

	The Most Common Idiomatic
The very nature of the stylized	*Uses*

idiomatic characteristics of the
brass section as orchestral instru-
ments precludes any systematic application of the *Reference Chart of
Keyboard Idioms and Patterns* as carried out for the strings and wood-
winds. However, certain entries of the *Reference Chart* have been examined in the surveys for each instrument. Others will be discussed in
the chapters devoted to scoring for full orchestra.

In planning orchestrations it is helpful to divide the brass section into
two units: (1) the horns, and (2) the trumpets, trombones, and tuba.
This division is pertinent because of the great diverse tonal strengths
and weights between these units, which affect scoring plans. The superior blending qualities of the horns has occasioned some musicologists
to associate them with the wood-winds rather than with the brass section. The remaining heavier brasses have the strongest timbres and
should therefore be reserved for passages requiring extra power, sonority,
and intensity.

The spectacular emergence of the brass section to a position of unprecedented dominance in the past century should be viewed in the context of changing trends in composition. These trends have led to an
ever-increasing emphasis on tonal brilliance and volume through expanded contrapuntal textures and harmonic vocabularies. Nonetheless,
a survey of orchestral scores from the early Classic period through the
twentieth century will reveal that the sensitive orchestrator has respected
orchestral values by differentiating between the appropriate and the in-

appropriate. To cite but one example: Ravel's scoring of his suite *Ma Mère l'oye* is entirely different from that for his choreographic poem *La Valse*. A perusal of the instrumentation for both works discloses their points of departure and intended scope.

The listing which follows summarizes the most common phases of scoring for the brass instruments either as an independent unit or in combination with the strings and wood-winds. The ten points should be integrated with the analysis given for each instrument so that they can become part of a practical scoring technique. They are closely allied to corresponding entries in the *Reference Chart of Keyboard Idioms and Patterns*.

1. Solo and octave melodic lines at all dynamic levels
2. Chordal progressions in choral style
3. Unisons, intervals, and chords used for percussive accents
4. Sustaining single notes, intervals, and chords at all dynamic levels
5. Rhythmic figurations
6. Outlining important melodies
7. Doubling strings and/or wood-winds in unison or octaves for extra emphasis and tonal strength
8. Increasing sonority for climaxes
9. As an independent section for contrasts in timbre and sonority
10. Coloristic effects

Representative excerpts for the brass section as an independent unit are given in Example B-34. They illustrate the section's aptness for chordal progressions horizontally conceived.

Example B-34

Example B-34 *(continued)*

Rimsky-Korsakov
Scheherazade

Franck
Symphony in D minor

Example B-34 *(continued)*

Example B-34 *(continued)*

Samuel Barber
Essay No. 1

By permission of G. Schirmer Co., New York. Copyright 1941.

Example B-34 *(continued)*

Hindemith
Mathis der Maler

Chapter 27

THE PERCUSSION SECTION

Percussion instruments are dissimilar in their pitch variance and vibrating characteristics. It is advisable and practical to consider them according to their respective categories.

*Percussion Instruments
  Classified According to
  Pitch and Timbre
Conventional Uses
Modern Adaptations*

1. **Pitch Variance**
    a. Instruments with Definite Pitch: timpani, chimes, glockenspiel (orchestra bells), xylophone, marimba, celeste,[1] and vibraphone.
    b. Instruments with Indefinite Pitch: snare drum (side drum), bass drum, cymbals, tambourine, triangle, wood block, castanets, tom-tom, temple blocks, gong, and tam-tam. **Note:** The last five were the least common in symphonic orchestration prior to the middle 1800's and are sometimes referred to as being "exotic," because of national associations.

2. **Vibrating Characteristics**
    a. Instruments Which Continue to Sound after Contact: timpani, chimes, glockenspiel, cymbals, triangle, gong, and tam-tam.
    b. Instruments Which Do Not Sound after Contact: xylophone, snare drum, bass drum, tambourine, wood block, temple blocks, and castanets. (Although the bass drum does have some continuing sound after being struck, its duration is not sufficient for classification with 2*a.*)

3. **Timbre:** A third category is that of timbre which is determined by the *kind* of vibrating surface: membrane, metal, or wood.
    a. Membrane: all types of drums, including the tambourine.
    b. Metal: glockenspiel, vibraphone, chimes, cymbals, triangle, gong, and tam-tam.
    c. Wood: wood block, temple blocks, xylophone, marimba, and castanets.

[1] See Chap. 33.

Instruments having *definite* pitch require a staff with a suitable clef. Those with *indefinite* pitch may be written on a staff or on a single line without any clef. Some composers have used the treble clef for the triangle and tambourine, but this practice is misleading and unnecessary.

The percussion instruments, as a section, were not used with any regularity until the close of the nineteenth century. Some isolated exceptions occur in the Haydn *Military* Symphony and the Mozart opera *Entführung aus dem Serail* where the triangle, cymbals, and bass drum are used primarily as coloristic devices.[1] Later, in the Finale of Beethoven's Ninth Symphony, these instruments served to heighten both the emotional and the rhythmic tension. Scoring for the section still adheres to these primary objectives.

Percussion instruments are of value only when they can add dimensions of timbre and nuance unobtainable from the other sections. Their inclusion should be judged, therefore, on their capacities to enliven, enrich, and heighten the musical values not obtainable from the other sections of the orchestra. They are strictly supplementary instruments with limited tonal definition which, in turn, affects their scoring values. This consideration is of especial significance in dealing with those instruments with indefinite pitch. The *type* of sound and its *frequency* are prime factors in evaluating their appropriateness at all times.

The unprecedented solo part for the triangle in the Liszt E flat Piano Concerto illustrates the desirability of choosing the right instrument for the right place. Here, its bell-like, percussive tone becomes an integral part of the over-all rhythmic design. Its appropriateness is ideal, as no other instrument could have matched its neutral, percussive effect.

Subtleties of percussive timbres are frequently lost by overwriting and overloading the parts, especially in loud *tuttis*. The opposite extreme of delicately stroked percussion has a piquant charm and color which is worth investigating. If percussion parts are well placed and spaced, their timbres can add extra dimensions of coloristic nuances that are singularly attractive. Rimsky-Korsakov said, in effect, "Students of orchestration first discover the percussion and gradually find the strings." It is wiser to reverse the order of discovery; for orchestration, as an art form, is not dependent upon the inclusion of percussion instruments, but does rely heavily upon good scoring for the strings.

Following are some of the more conventional ways of using percussion instruments at all dynamic levels.

1. Establishing and maintaining rhythmic *ostinatos*. These are best suited to instruments with indefinite pitch.

2. Outlining melodic ideas and figurations. In this category *definite*-pitched instruments are the more effective. Those with *indefinite* pitch are useful in heightening pulsation and adding volume and intensity.

---

[1] The use of the percussion in these two examples shows each composer's intention of adding an "exotic" touch by imitating Turkish military bands.

3. Group scoring of mixed-percussion timbres, either separately or in combination with other sections, increases rhythmic vitality and/or volume while contributing the means of contrast.

4. Coloristic rhythmic effects derived from the design of principal melodic ideas have continuity and interest.

5. Short color splashes, with or without rhythmic pulsation, highlight nuances momentarily.

6. As an independent rhythm section with diversified inner rhythmic patterns.

7. For pointing up the apex in tonal climaxes.

8. For the effect of long, sustained percussive sound. Rolls on the snare drum, bass drum, cymbal, or triangle are the most common in this category.

9. For short, quick piling up of sound.

10. For carrying out rhythmic patterns not practicable in the other sections of the orchestra.

Chapter 28

VIBRATION CHARACTERISTICS

Notation Problems Due to This Cause

The vibrating characteristics of percussion instruments are totally different from those of the other sections which, in turn, accounts for specific problems affecting their notation. Instruments made of metal continue to sound or ring in varying degrees after contact. Those made of wood and two of the drum group, the snare drum and the tambourine, cease vibrating immediately after contact. Only the timpani in the percussion group has continuing resonance of any consequence.

The effect of these vibrating characteristics on the notation of percussion instruments made of metal is illustrated in Fig. P-1a.

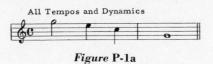

Figure P-1a

If this notation is used for a xylophone or marimba, the resulting sound would be notated as follows:

Figure P-1b

For instruments with non-vibrating surfaces with indefinite pitch, the sounding notation is as given in Fig. P-1c.

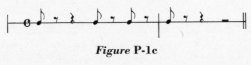

Figure P-1c

253

If the *effect* of continuous tone is required for instruments made of wood with definite pitch, the notation should read as follows:

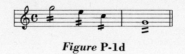

Figure **P-1d**

Notation for the other instruments in this category, but with *indefinite* pitch, is written in this manner:

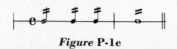

Figure **P-1e**

To summarize: Percussion instruments made of metal do not require any form of tremolo. Those made of wood and the two drum types previously noted can maintain continuous sound only by means of some form of repeated attacks.

Note: The notation indicating double strokes in Figs. P-1d and P-1e is acceptable for tempos of *allegro* or faster. All slower tempos should have triple flags.

Chapter 29

THE DRUM GROUP

THE TIMPANI

(Fr. *timbales;* It. *timpani;*
Ger. *Pauken*)

Timpani
Snare Drum
Bass Drum
Tambourine
Tom-tom

Kettledrums, best known by their Italian name, timpani, are referred to in the plural because they are invariably used in pairs. These copper-kettle-shaped drums with calfskin heads are made in two types: hand-tuned and the newer pedal-tuned. The hand-tuned, which was standard until the early 1900s, has a set of evenly spaced handles around the edges of the rim. One-half turn for each of these handles alters the pitch by approximately one semitone. This technicality accounts for the necessity of allowing sufficient time for pitch changes during performance. The hand-tuned type naturally needs longer rest intervals than does the pedal timpani, on which pitch changes can be made almost instantaneously.

In dealing with practical orchestration, it is advisable to write for the hand-tuned drums and to arrange the parts accordingly, as the pedal type is not consistently available. The range compass of a pair of timpani covers an octave for both types. The larger drum is always placed at the player's left. Supplementary larger and smaller timpani are standard with major orchestras but they are practically nonexistent in school and amateur ensembles.

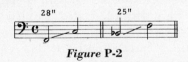

Figure P-2

Timpani sticks are made of wood with mallet heads ranging from soft to hard. Considerable variation in sound and attack can be obtained through the interchange of sticks, which choice is usually left to the discretion of the player or conductor. Stick technique employs single strokes with alternating hands for rolls and the more common rhythmic patterns. A skilled timpanist is a specialist, capable of performing surprising feats in applying stick technique to as many as four drums. A timpanist rarely doubles on other percussion instruments.

Classical composers usually scored for timpani in pairs invariably tuned to the tonic and dominant, but always with a C major notation, as was the case for the natural horns and trumpets. (See Example B-8a.) In post-Classical times, composers indicated a more accurate notation by writing correct pitches but omitting accidentals, except tunings, at the beginning of each movement. (See Example B-8b.) It was not until the close of the nineteenth century that composers began using accidentals in timpani parts. Since then some attempts have been made to include key signatures as a means of standardization. These experiments have, in general, been resolved by writing the exact notation, including accidentals in the parts as they occur, but omitting key signatures. Figure P-3 illustrates the above-mentioned practices for timpani notation.

Notation Styles

PITCH SETTINGS FOR TUNING

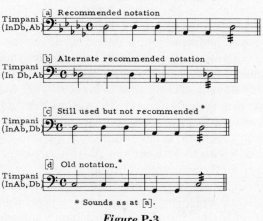

* Sounds as at [a].

Figure P-3

Although the resonance from the timpani is actively vibrant, *continuous* tone is possible only with the roll. All rolled notes which are not tied should theoretically receive fresh attacks, as with the other instruments. This technicality of notation is present in scores prior to the early 1900s. Any possible confusion with this detail can be eliminated by indicating clearly the starting and stopping points of all rolls.

Notation for all rolled notes may be written in either of the two ways

given in Fig. P-4a and b. Rolled intervals for one player are practicable
if confined to two drums (Fig. P-4c).

Figure P-4

Timpani notation can be precise for tone durations and playing styles.
Timpani resonance can be controlled by applying the finger tips to the
drum head, which stops or chokes off the tone. Playing styles admit the
full gamut of dynamics for accents, *staccato* strokes, and rolls.

Orchestral Usage

Timpani parts in early Classic scores were quite stylized. They were
frequently combined with horns and trumpets as the major means of
securing maximum sonority and brilliance. As previously referred to
(Examples B-8a and b), this instrumental combination figured prominently in climaxes and at strong cadences. Some of the last scores of
Haydn and Mozart show some deviation from this usage, but it remained for Beethoven's audacious originality to exploit the timpani in
heretofore untried paths. His nine symphonies show a progressive independence of the timpani for solo parts of interest and significance. Some
typical examples of these parts follow:

Example P-1

Example P-1 *(continued)*

Example P-1a is interesting because of its use of the timpani as an independent bass part. The following example from Tchaikovsky's Fourth Symphony illustrates the use of the same device half a century later.

Example P-2

A further development of Beethoven's solo octaves in Example P-1c is to be found in the opening measures of the *Scherzo* movement by Sibelius, which has the timpani playing the rhythmic pattern of the main theme.

Example P-3

Berlioz' unprecedented scoring for four solo timpani to suggest distant thunder in the Pastoral movement of his *Symphonie fantastique* introduced an imaginative concept never before exploited thus.

Example P-4

The following list summarizes the timpani's most common playing assets and uses:

1. For building climaxes either with a roll or for the repetition of a rhythmic figure not necessarily doubled by other instruments.

2. For emphasis in all forms: melodically, harmonically, and rhythmically.

3. When played *staccato,* it is not unlike the *pizzicato* of cello and bass.

4. Particularly effective when combined with the brass, either full or in part.

5. For solo snatches of thematic bits, often arranged antiphonally.

6. For outlining the pulsations of bass *ostinatos.*

7. In long, sustained rolls as pedal points for either *crescendos* or *diminuendos.*

8. In intervals—played together or broken.

9. For creation of tension through the use of *ostinatos,* preferably derived from the rhythmic pattern of principal thematic ideas.

Inasmuch as the timpani have been an integral part of the orchestra practically since its inception, the student orchestrator should consider them as musical instruments and not as supplementary "noise makers." Although percussive to a degree, they do not belong to the same category as the other percussion instruments, which are decidedly more limited and prescribed in their usage.

THE SNARE DRUM

(Fr. *caisse claire* (or *tambour*); It. *cassa* (or *tamburo*); Ger. *Trommel*)

The lack of any standardization of these drums often poses a problem for the orchestrator, conductor, and player because of their variations in size and sonority. However, the model used for orchestral work in America is about 6 inches deep with two membrane heads some 14 or 15 inches in diameter. A set of snares (wire-covered gut strings) are attached to a clamping device which regulates their tension and contact with the bottom drum head. The movement of these snares on the bottom head accounts for its bright, *secco*[1] tone. If the snares are released, the resulting sound becomes similar to that of an Indian tom-tom or other folk-type drum.

The roll, unlike that of the timpani, is double-stroked and frequently ends on an accent. Notation is much the same as that given for the timpani. The termination of rolls can be clearly indicated by tying rolled notes to an unrolled note, as in Fig. P-5. This method of notation is correct for rolls on all percussion instruments.

Figure P-5

Two styles of stick technique, the "flam" and the "drag," apply only to the snare drum. Both prefix one or more grace notes to basic notations. Most orchestrators usually leave the choice of stroke to the player's discretion. The difference between written and sounding notations resulting from these styles is illustrated in the conventional roll-off (Fig. P-6).

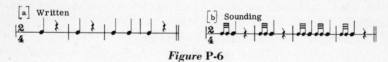

Figure P-6

The snare drum, in symphonic orchestration, has limited values and assets. Nineteenth-century composers used it almost exclusively for martial music (Liszt's *Les Préludes—tempo di marcia*) and the afterbeats in dance forms. Notable exceptions occur in the "March to the Scaffold" movement in the *Symphonie fantastique* by Berlioz and in the final climax of the Strauss symphonic poem *Till Eulenspiegel*. In these passages both composers called for large military drums to depict a mood of impending doom. Latter-day composers have found the snare drum useful in giving percussive verve to important rhythmic figurations (Debussy's *Fêtes*), in maintaining endless *ostinatos* (Ravel's *Bolero*), and for building grandiose climaxes (Aaron Copland's *Outdoor Overture*). Other composers have found novel uses for it in the softer dynamic

---

[1] Dry, hard, brittle.

levels, which are fascinating in timbre and design (Ravel's *Rhapsodie espagnole;* Prokofiev's Symphony No. 5; Bartók's Concerto for Orchestra).

Several special effects have been introduced to vary the snare drum's normal characteristic timbre. In addition to the tom-tom drum with released snares, these include: muffled head (cloth covering the "batter" head), playing with wire-spread brushes or timpani sticks and rim shots (striking one stick against a second stick in contact with the batter head and metal rim to produce pistol-like reports).

The snare drum should not be used indiscriminately for loud *tuttis* and endings, as is the case with much band music. Its clear, crisp tone loses its effectiveness if overprolonged in music for the orchestra.

THE BASS DRUM

(Fr. *grosse caisse;* It. *cassa, gran cassa;* Ger. *grosse Trommel*)

The bass drum is a "noise maker" par excellence with a booming resonance of great carrying power which is in proportion to its size. The usual symphony model has two membrane heads about 30 inches in diameter and a wood shell with a depth of some 16 inches.

Notation and playing techniques are similar to that for the timpani with one exception. A single bass-drum beater, or stick, with a large, moderately hard head is used ordinarily. If timpani sticks are to be substituted, directions should include the kind of head desired: soft, medium, or hard.

Historically, the bass drum has been invariably paired with the cymbals. This combination persisted well into the middle of the nineteenth century, when composers began to recognize the values to be derived from their occasional separation. One such advantage is the bass-drum roll, with its ominous deep thud. Others include short strokes for rhythmic, dynamic, and coloristic effects, either alone or in combination with the other percussion instruments. A much-abused and overworked instrument in the late 1900s, its effect is in inverse ratio to the frequency of its appearances in a score—the fewer notes the better!

THE TAMBOURINE

(Fr. *tambour de Basque;* It. *tamburo basco, tamburino;*
Ger. *Schellentrommel, Tamburin*)

The orchestral tambourine has a diameter of about 10 inches, but with only one drum head, and is equipped with a set of small metal disks called jingles. These jingles are set in pairs and vibrate in proportion to the movement of the instrument.

Several playing styles are used. For percussive strokes on the drum head, the player uses either his fist or knuckles. Different kinds of drum sticks are sometimes substituted. Continuous rolls of the jingles are made either by shaking the instrument or by using a highly specialized technique of rubbing a moistened thumb around the edges of the drum head. Neither style produces any percussive sound from the drum head. A continuous percussive roll can be made only with drum sticks. The tambourine is frequently paired with the triangle because of its high-pitched jingles.

Orchestral parts for the tambourine have generally carried connotations of the "exotic" but this association is not entirely justified. Actually, its dual percussive characteristics can add zest and verve to music which is rhythmic, gay, colorful, and festive. It is a kind of miniature drum with jingles, capable of splash-color effects at all dynamic levels.

Chapter 30

PERCUSSION INSTRUMENTS MADE OF METAL

Triangle
Cymbals
Glockenspiel
Vibraphone
Chimes
Gong
Tam-tam
Antique Cymbals

THE TRIANGLE

(Fr. *triangle;* It. *triangolo;* Ger. *Triangel*)

The triangle is a small steel bar bent in the shape of a triangle, but with one open end. The standard orchestra size is about 6½ inches on a side. A small steel rod is used as a beater. Short rhythmic patterns and tremolos are common at all dynamic levels. Its bright, high-pitched, bell-like tone has piquant charm if used judiciously. A few well-chosen strokes can enliven soft dance measures or a powerful *tutti*. Its brilliance is therefore the key to estimating the scope of its effectiveness. Representative parts for the triangle, without other percussion instruments, are to be found in the following symphonies: Schumann No. 1, Brahms No. 4, Dvořák No. 5, and Tchaikovsky No. 4.

THE CYMBALS
(Fr. *cymbales;* It. *piatti;* Ger. *Becken*)

Cymbal resonance and tonal strength vary with size and quality. The preferred orchestral sizes for symphonic ensembles range from 15 to 18 inches in diameter. Turkish cymbals, made of a brass alloy, have long been favored for their superior vibrating qualities. Matched pairs, played manually, are supplemented by a third, suspended cymbal for use with different kinds of drum sticks.

The normal playing style calls for glancing blows of paired cymbals which, contrary to casual observation, are equally effective *pianissimo* as well as *fortissimo*. The heretofore old technique of rubbing cymbals together for rolls has been displaced by the more controllable one employing sticks on a suspended cymbal. In the latter form, directions should include the type of sticks to be used: wood, metal, or timpani. Omitting this information can lead to distortion of the part.

Notation for cymbals in the twentieth century has become more accurately detailed than previously. Standard notation has, in general, been supplanted by diamond-shaped notes which give better visual definition, especially when they share the same staff with the bass drum. Notation has also become more precise in indicating cymbal resonance. Tone can be stopped almost instantaneously by bringing the cymbals in contact with wearing apparel, indicated by the word "dampen" or "choke." A hand is used to "choke" a suspended cymbal. If the cymbals are to continue vibrating after contact beyond the limits of notation for a given measure, the words "allow to vibrate" or *"laisser vibrer"* are written in the part.

Loud cymbal crashes should be withheld for peak moments of climaxes with tonal and rhythmic tension, as their explosive power palls quickly. A few well-placed and spaced crashes (Tchaikovsky's *Romeo and Juliet,* middle *Allegro* section) have real strength and character. Repeated crashes (final measures of Tchaikovsky's Symphony No. 4) tend to degenerate into mere noise which obscures tonal balance without increasing musical values.

THE GLOCKENSPIEL
(Fr. *jeu de timbres, carillon;* It. *campanella;* Ger. *Glockenspiel*)

The glockenspiel, more commonly known as orchestra bells, is a set of chromatically pitched steel bars arranged in a playing position similar to that of the piano keyboard. It is written in the treble clef and is a transposing instrument. The writing of signatures, though optional, is recommended. Since tonal ranges vary with the size of each instrument, the following compass is given as a practicable, safe compromise. **Note:** The sounding range is *two octaves higher* than the written one.

Figure **P-7**

The glockenspiel was originally played with a keyboard (Mozart's opera *The Magic Flute*). It has since been supplanted by a manual technique employing mallets held in the hands of the player. This newer method has the advantage of a greater dynamic range inasmuch as different kinds of mallet heads can be used: yarn, rubber, wood, or metal. The choice of mallet heads is usually left to the player, the selection being determined by the dynamic of each passage. Single notes, intervals, and three-note chords are playable if confined to an octave.

The instrument has a bright, brilliant sonority with good carrying power. Accumulated, undampened vibrations from many notes produce a tonal blurring which is, in this case, a characteristic asset. Its luminous resonance minimizes any dryly percussive sound. Relatively short solo melodic phrases have a distinctive charm in the soft–to–medium-loud dynamic range levels (The Dance of the Apprentices in Richard Wagner's *Die Meistersinger* and the *Scherzo* from Rachmaninov's Second Symphony). Its tone is well suited to outlining melodic and rhythmic ideas, for short color dabs of single notes or intervals, and for splashy *glissandos* on very rapid *crescendos*. The instrument does not respond too well to rapid double strokes.

Figure P-8

THE VIBRAPHONE

The vibraphone is an extra-large glockenspiel equipped with resonators, each containing revolving disks operated electrically. These resonators produce an exaggerated *vibrato* which, in turn, causes continuous blurring and overlapping of successive tones. The almost exclusive use of soft mallet heads precludes any dynamics beyond those in the softer levels. Rapid passages, though technically possible, are tonally unsatisfactory if any degree of clarity is wished. It has a four-octave range starting on small-octave C. This newest member of the percussion section has been used in orchestrations of "entertainment" music, but as yet, it has made little progress in the field of symphonic composition. Morton Gould has included the vibraphone in the scores of his *Spirituals* and *Latin-American Symphonette*.

THE CHIMES

(Fr. *cloches;* It. *campane;* Ger. *Glocken*)

The chimes are perhaps most familiar as part of the percussion section of bands. They consist of a set of long tubular metal pipes and are usually hung on a specially constructed rack or frame. Their range covers an octave and a perfect fourth, with intervening chromatics as follows:

Figure P-9

A gavel-like hammer is used for single strokes. Successive tones pile up jangling overtones similar to that of a carillon. As these large bells speak slowly, it is advisable to avoid fast-moving notations. Single strokes, well spaced, give the most satisfactory results.

Bell tones, either real or imitated, have always fascinated composers. This is to be noted more particularly in orchestral works of the nineteenth century. In the Carillon movement of Bizet's *L'Arlésienne* Suite No. 1, the composer has set up a 52-measure imitated bell *ostinato*. A similar but less potent imitation occurs in the Angelus section of Massenet's *Scènes pittoresques*. Berlioz, in the final section of his *Symphonie fantastique,* wrote for two chimes and six pianos!

Kodály has combined chimes cleverly with other percussive instruments in his witty *Háry János* Suite (Example P-7). A comparison of real and imitative clanging church-bell sounds can be found in the Coronation Scene in Moussorgsky's opera, *Boris Godunov* and the *Russian Easter* Overture by Rimsky-Korsakov. The realistic effect of chimes have glowing color in the final movements of *Iberia* by Debussy and by Albéniz in the Arbós transcription.

THE TAM-TAM AND THE GONG

The tam-tam is of Far Eastern origin and is rightly scored most infrequently. This large bronze disk measures some 28 inches in diameter and has a turned-down rim to minimize its high vibration frequency. A smaller type, known as a gong, is frequently substituted for the larger tam-tam. Both instruments have a strong low-pitched resonance and tonal power which limit their usefulness. Single strokes with a large beater are rarely used softer than *mezzo-forte*.

Nineteenth-century composers seem to have associated the tam-tam with moods of gloom and despair (Tchaikovsky's Symphony No. 6). Later composers, however, have scored it in various ways: as a super-cymbal (George Gershwin's Concerto in F); for its coloristic potential (Example P-7); and for its sheer overwhelming tonal strength, as found in the final movements of *Pictures at an Exhibition* (Moussorgsky-Ravel) and *The Pines of Rome* (Respighi).

THE ANTIQUE CYMBALS

(Fr. *crotales;* It. *crotali;* Ger. *antiken Zimpeln*)

Antique cymbals are tiny discs made in pairs, with definite pitch. They are held in the palm of the hands by small straps which permit them to ring after their rims have been struck together. These bell-like cymbals are rather impractical, as their pitch variance has never been standardized. Because of the difficulty of obtaining these cymbals, orchestral bells are substituted. Debussy wrote briefly for them in the final measures of his *L'Après-midi d'un faune.* Parts for antique cymbals with differing pitches have been used by Berlioz in his *Roméo et Juliette,* by Ravel in *Daphnis et Chloé,* and by Stravinsky in *Le Sacre du printemps.*

Chapter 31

PERCUSSION INSTRUMENTS MADE OF WOOD

THE XYLOPHONE

(Fr. *xylophone;* It. *xilofono;*
Ger. *Xylophon*)

The xylophone differs from the
glockenspiel in that its bars are
made of wood instead of metal.

Xylophone
Marimba
Wood Block
Temple Blocks
Castanets

There are two types: a folding set without resonators with a small-to-moderate range, and a more elaborate set mounted on a special frame with resonators having a chromatic compass of more than three octaves. The latter is the exception rather than the rule. The treble clef is used for the varying ranges as follows:

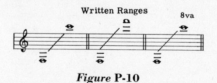

Figure P-10

The xylophone sounds an *octave higher* than written. Playing technique is approximately the same as for the glockenspiel, with an interchange of mallets available for dynamic variance. Its tone is dry, brittle, and percussive. Slow melodies require a constant tremolo and are not successful. Its best parts include short solos of rhythmic-melodic interest, outlining rapid figurations, accenting melodic and harmonic elements, and arpeggiated chords. Short, quick *glissandos,* which end on an accented note, add color splashes. Intervals and three-note chords are practicable. Some representative passages for xylophone can be seen in context in the following scores:

Saint-Saëns, *Danse macabre*
Prokofiev, *Scythian Suite*
Howard Hanson, *Merry Mount* Suite
Douglas Moore, *Pageant of P. T. Barnum*
Kabalevsky, *Colas Breugnon* Suite
Lambert, *The Rio Grande*
Gardner Read, First Overture
Joseph Wagner, Symphony No. 1

THE MARIMBA

The marimba is an elaborate model of the xylophone, with a characteristic subdued, mellow tone usually played with soft-head mallets. Instruments in this country have a four-octave compass and are equipped with resonators. Those in Latin America are made large enough to allow four or five players to function as a unit. The marimba has not as yet been used by symphonic composers with sufficient regularity to warrant detailed comment. It is not easily available and is therefore an impractical percussion instrument for scoring purposes.

THE WOOD BLOCK

The wood block is a hollowed-out, rectangular piece of wood with slots on each side near the top playing surface. Snare-drum sticks or hard xylophone mallets are used with single stroke attacks to point up accents and rhythmic patterns and for dry, brittle, isolated tappings designed specifically for neutral percussive effects. Although Chinese in origin, the wood block has become an almost exclusive American adaptation. Parts for it are included in the following works:

Aaron Copland's suites, *Billy the Kid* and *Rodeo*
George Gershwin, Concerto in F
Prokofiev, Symphony No. 5
Ravel, *Concerto for the Left Hand*
Joseph Wagner, Suite, *Hudson River Legend*
Walton, Suite from *Façade*

TEMPLE BLOCKS

Temple blocks, also Chinese in origin, are round, brightly lacquered wooden blocks, usually five in number and roughly tuned to approximate the notes of a pentatonic scale. Various sticks and mallets are used with resulting sounds resembling those associated with gourds of different sizes. Temple blocks, long-familiar sounds in dance bands, have not found their way into many symphonic scores. Two exceptions occur in Morton Gould's *Latin-American Symphonette* and Howard Hanson's suite, *Merry Mount*. Notation is with "x's" at various pitch levels without clefs.

THE CASTANETS

Castanets are shell-shaped pieces of hard wood made in pairs. They are fastened together by string which is loose enough to permit manipulation by the fingers when held in the palm of the hands. However, as this style of playing requires a quite highly developed skill, castanets are more frequently fastened to a wooden paddle which permits them to be played in the manner of a rattle or clapper.

Castanets have always seemed to carry connotations of Spanish or Latin-American dance music, clicking out rhythms neatly and adding local color. European composers of serious music have used them occasionally without these connotations. A notable example occurs in the "Paris" version of the Bacchanale in Richard Wagner's opera *Tannhäuser*. Ravel also used them in his ballet *Daphnis et Chloé*.

Chapter 32

THE PERCUSSION ENSEMBLE

Not until the turn of the twentieth century did composers free themselves from the conventions of scoring percussion ensembles chiefly for the accentuation of music's elemental rhythmic figures and pulsations. Up to that time there was only slight interplay of independent rhythmic patterns within the section. It was customary to have the lighter instruments (triangle, tambourine, and snare drum) playing together on rhythms taken from the melodic line. The heavier ones (cymbals and bass drum) were used to emphasize the rhythmic pulse of harmonic progressions and/or strong beats of the measures. Likewise, there was an absence of experimentation of percussive timbres and their coloristic potentials in the softer dynamic levels.

More recent composers have expanded the scope of the section beyond these practices. They have recognized and differentiated between pitch levels, timbres, and tonal strengths of each instrument. Their unanimity of interest in the importance of the rhythmic vitality of music brought about a more diversified arrangement of percussion parts with an interplay of mixed rhythmic patterns within the section. Yet, in so doing, the primary objectives of color and tension have not been lost or sacrificed. Last, but not least, has been their advanced accomplishments with percussion instruments at the softer dynamic levels. Here, percussive timbres have become more subtle, provocative, and attractive. This newer concept added a new dimension of *timbre sonorities*.

It is of more than passing interest to note that very few scorings of the full percussion ensemble in orchestral *tuttis* include percussive instruments with definite pitch other than the timpani. Rather, they do combine instruments with various indefinite pitch levels and place them according to the most salient characteristics of the music. The following excerpts are devoted to the percussion ensemble for the purpose of illustrating the gradual development of independent parts for the section within a relatively short period of time. (The Britten excerpt, Example P-8, is for the percussion as a solo unit.)

Example P-5

Example P-6

Example P-6 *(continued)*

Example P-7

Example P-8

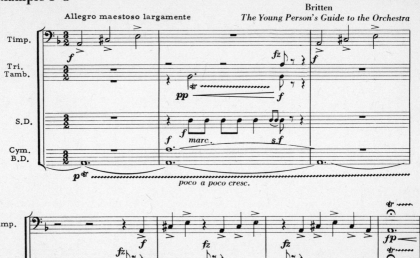

By permission of Boosey and Hawkes, Inc., New York and London.

Chapter 33

SUPPLEMENTARY INSTRUMENTS

THE HARP

(Fr. *harpe;* It. *arpa;* Ger. *Harfe*)

Harp
Celesta
Piano
Organ

The improved nineteenth-century chromatic harp was a major advancement over the earlier *diatonic* instrument of the Classic period. (For the latter see Mozart's Concerto for Flute, Harp and Orchestra, Beethoven's ballet *Prometheus,* and Berlioz' *Symphonie fantastique.*) However, this harp has been supplanted by a more recent diatonic, double-action instrument which now has become standard. It permits reasonably quick chromatic changes which were impractical with the two older instruments. The double-action harp is tuned in the key of Cb major and has the following compass:

Figure **H-1**

Pitch changes are made by seven foot pedals which operate a ratchet mechanism. These pedal positions carry through pitch changes from the normally tuned flat (b) starting point to semitone positions of natural (♮) and sharp (♯) positions, thereby completing the chromatic cycle throughout the full compass of the instrument.

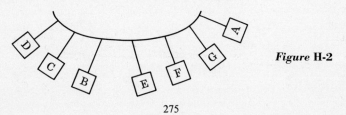

Figure **H-2**

Pedal changes can be made quite rapidly without serious interruption of the rhythmic flow of the part. A harpist does have the problem of marking pedal changes for each new piece in advance of rehearsals. Some orchestrators include major pedal changes in the part, but most harpists prefer to do their own editing.

Orchestral harp parts were, for two centuries, rather stereotyped, rarely deviating from simple *arpeggios* and chords. Example H-1 illustrates these playing styles as taken from the score of *Les Préludes* by Liszt. The doubling of the harp with wood-winds on a secondary theme was something of an innovation but is now a common practice (Example H-1b).

Example H-1

Totally new styles of harp technique were introduced in the works of the French Impressionists Debussy and Ravel and their contemporaries. They included enharmonics, *glissandos,* blocked chords, trills, tremolos, and occasional solo passages. Most of these innovations are well represented in Debussy's *Danse sacrée et danse profane* and in Ravel's *Introduction et allegro* for harp, flute, clarinet, and string quartet.

Twentieth-century composers have extended the scope of orchestral harp parts largely through the extraordinary experiments made by the eminent harpist-composer, Carlos Salzedo. His unprecedented new playing techniques are fully recorded in the Salzedo-Lawrence, *Method for Harp.* The future will, no doubt, see these idiomatic devices included in orchestral harp parts.

Notation for the harp is essentially the same as that for the piano, with a few exceptions. These differences are the result of idiomatic harp techniques, most of which are not playable on the piano. They are summarized as follows:

1. The harpist does not use the fifth finger of either hand. Unbroken chords for each hand should therefore not exceed an octave. Chords are rolled or broken slightly in conventional playing and rolled upwards unless indicated otherwise. A bracket ([) is placed before all chords which are to be played together non-*arpeggiato.* Chords may be rolled in opposite directions by adding arrows to the regular wavy lines. Chords, rolled through with both hands, may start with either the top or bottom notes. These playing styles are listed in Fig. H-3.

Figure **H-3**

2. Enharmonics are idiomatic for repeated notes playable by both hands (Figs. H-4 and H-5).

Figure **H-4**

The use of *enharmonics* increases resonance and they can be written in many ways which are idiomatically desirable to facilitate fingerings.

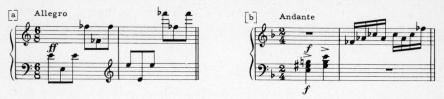

Figure **H-5**

3. The harp, because of its tuning to C♭ major, is more adaptable to flat keys than those in sharps. Enharmonic notes and keys are therefore preferable when practicable. For example, C♭ major is preferable to B major.

4. *Pentatonic* scales (five notes), formed with enharmonics, give the most resonance for *glissandos,* intervals, and/or chords (example: F–G–A♯–B♭–C–D–E♯). *Glissandos* may be for single notes, intervals, or chords. Their two styles of notation are given in Fig. H-6.

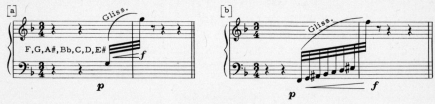

Figure **H-6**

Glissandos extending over many beats have varying notations, depending upon the tempo in which they occur. Their sweeping strokes are indicated approximately rather than accurately.

Figure **H-7**

The up-stroke *glissando* (*crescendo*) is, according to Walter Piston, "one of the worst platitudes of music." The down-stroke style (*diminuendo*) occurs much less frequently.

(a) Harmonics are written where played.

Figure H-8

5. Harmonics are a coloristic device with weak carrying strength. They are played by plucking the upper half of the string after it has been stopped at one-half of its length. Since this is a technique done by one hand, it is unwise to write successive harmonics too rapidly. Notation for harmonics requires a circle (○) placed directly over the pitch to be stopped. The resulting sound will be *one octave higher* than the written note. Harpists differ in their preference for the notation of harmonics; some like the actual pitch to be indicated. A directive in the part explaining the style used will avoid all possible confusion.

Harmonics for single notes and small intervals in the middle register have the best resonance and are playable by one or both hands. They may be played by both hands or divided, as in Fig. H-8. Harmonics are especially attractive with wood-winds and only slightly less so with strings.

6. Harp trills and tremolos are of less value than those for the piano. They are slowed down somewhat in playing and are comparatively infrequent in orchestral scores.

Although trills can be played with either hand, they are more satisfactory when notated for both hands.

Figure H-9

Tremolos (*bisbigliando*—"whispering") employ both hands to keep the strings constantly in motion. Soft dynamics for three or four notes, within an octave, are playable. Some composers have written tremolos at louder levels, as given in Fig. H-10b.

Figure H-10

Harp resonance is not entirely conducive to long, sustained melodic lines unless confined to the middle register. These notes are satisfactory whether alone or doubling other instruments. The lowest bass tones have good resonance with considerable tonal strength. The harp sounds well with the strings but is clearer, by contrast, when scored with wind instruments.

THE CELESTA

The celesta has tonal similarities to the glockenspiel but is equipped with a piano-type keyboard and a damper pedal. It is generally classified as a percussion instrument, as its tone is produced by felt hammers striking steel bars placed on a wooden frame. In appearance it resembles a small harmonium or spinet piano. Its tone is light, thin, and subdued—qualities quite removed from the more brilliant glockenspiel. Although the full range of dynamics is used, the actual degree of change is quite slight.

Notation is the same as that for the piano, with the treble and bass clefs used on one or two staves as required. It is a transposing instrument with the sounding notes being *one octave higher* than the written ones. The full compass is as follows:

Figure **C-1**

The keyboard action is unusually responsive, enabling the player to execute rapid passages with comparative ease. Its bell-like tones, played *forte,* have approximately one-half the tonal strength of the glockenspiel, played with hard rubber hammers. The celesta tone will, however, be slightly more incisive. The depressed damper pedal increases resonance by the free play of the accumulated vibrations. As its strongest tone can be smothered by heavier orchestral sonorities, it is advisable to have the significant parts well exposed.

The celesta is rarely available in secondary orchestras. A piano playing an octave higher than written, is frequently used as the most practical substitution. The resultant loss is one of tonal delicacy, charm, and character.

The celesta's tone and playing styles are readily adaptable for musical ornamentation. These may take the form of arabesque figurations, scales, chords, *arpeggios,* doublings with wood-winds and/or muted strings, and occasional solo passages with melodic interest. Its tone quality has good blending potentials with the other orchestral instruments.

As celesta parts are frequently quite meaningless out of context, the orchestrator should examine parts for it in the following scores:

Bartók, *Music for Piano, Celesta, Percussion, and Strings*
Dukas, *La Péri*
Holst, *The Planets*
Ibert, *Escales*
Ravel, *Ma Mère l'oye*
Gardner Read, *Sketches of the City*
Tchaikovsky, *Nutcracker* Suite

THE PIANO
(Fr. *piano;* It. *pianoforte;* Ger. *Klavier*)

As the technique of the piano—its range, sonority, and resources—are familiar to all students of music, it remains only to be evaluated in terms of an orchestral instrument.

The piano's prototype, the harpsichord, was used in the seventeenth century for "realizations" of figured bass parts. This highly specialized form of improvisation was intended to strengthen bass parts, to "fill in" the middle harmonic gaps, and to act as a steadying influence for the ensemble. These "realizations" had the left hand doubling the bass part while the right hand moved somewhat independently with harmonizations but without doubling the top melodic lines. A sample of this style of writing may be advantageously examined in the Kalmus edition of Corelli's Concerto Grosso No. 8 (*Christmas*), which has both the "realization" and the figured bass part. It is a utilitarian style of writing which can serve as a model for average scorings of small orchestral ensembles. A more modern and greatly expanded style of piano writing is to be found in Manuel de Falla's effective score for small orchestra, *El Amor Brujo*. In both works the harpsichord and the piano respectively are used orchestrally, but the scope in style and relative importance between the two parts is enormous. The Falla score shows most clearly the unique characteristic possibilities of the piano as a quasi-solo, *obbligato* instrument. In this instance the orchestrator should examine closely not only the technical aspects, but the context of the settings as well. The composer wisely refrained from using the piano continuously.

The piano as an orchestral instrument has figured prominently in the scores of many twentieth-century composers who eliminated the harp almost completely from their scores. This has been a change of emphasis resulting from a different and newer set of musical values which strives to accentuate novel rhythmical and percussive characteristics. The piano's dry, percussive tone fits well into this predominately nonlyrical style of composition for many types of doubling, outlining, and figure elaboration. It is, in this respect, an extra means of tonal strength and emphasis. Sustained *cantabile* melodies, so conspicuous in earlier periods, are intentionally omitted as being ineffectual. The goal is toward greater brilliance, with passage work often reaching virtuoso grades of difficulty.

Since the piano as an orchestral instrument divorced from its musical context, is inconclusive, the orchestrator can obtain practical guidance from the scores listed below.

Samuel Barber, *First Essay*
Aaron Copland, *El Salon Mexico, Outdoor Overture, Rodeo*
Paul Creston, *Two Choric Dances*
Hindemith, *The Four Temperaments*
Kodály, suite, *Háry János*
Shostakovitch, Symphony No. 1
Stravinsky, ballet, *Petrouchka*

Composers of the nineteenth century tried the experiment of writing for the piano as a quasi-solo, *obbligato* instrument with orchestra. These scores call for a virtuoso technique but integrate the solo part into the orchestral texture with a minimum of artificial display passages. Some representative scores in this classification are:

D'Indy, *Symphony on a Mountain Air*
Franck, symphonic poem, *Les Djinns*
Loeffler, *Pagan Poem*
Saint-Saëns, Symphony No. 3 (two and four hands)

THE ORGAN

The organ, often referred to as "the king of instruments," is a "self-sufficient" keyboard instrument with a non-percussive tone. Its greatest assets are in sustaining tone at all dynamic levels with a great variety of timbres and in projecting its own tremendous power and brilliance.

There are two distinct and separate keyboard units. The principal one, the manuals for the fingers, vary in number with each instrument, three banks, or rows, being average. Each has a standardized compass, as follows:

Figure OR-1

The foot pedals are arranged similarly to the manuals and can be tonally augmented from the manuals by couplers. Their compass is as follows:

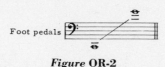

Figure **OR-2**

Organ parts have been frequently included in orchestrations of cantatas, oratorios, and operas with religious connotations dating back to the Baroque period. Solo concertos with orchestral accompaniment have also been fairly numerous. However, it was the nineteenth-century composers who brought the organ into symphonic instrumentation, but with a rather different intent. Their interest and purpose was to increase tonal dimensions of timbre and power beyond the extremes attainable with regular instrumentation. This newer concept is well illustrated in scores which have prolonged, sustained pedal notes and the full organ on massive climaxes. The organ is well equipped to handle these demands as its very construction provides for multiple combinations of stops and couplers which insure both variety of timbre and tonal strength along with unlimited capacity for *sostenuto*. Because it is an instrument distinctly apart from all the others, its use orchestrally requires considerable familiarity with its technicalities and tonal characteristics.

One ever-present difficulty in writing for the organ with orchestra is its uncertain availability and quality. Although most concert halls usually have good instruments, some used for orchestral performances are not always so equipped. The orchestrator should recognize this condition and be prepared to have an organ part either omitted or perhaps played on an electronic instrument.

The following scores are recommended as source material for the study of the organ as both a solo and supplementary orchestral instrument.

Bach-Respighi, Passacaglia and Fugue in C minor
Holst, *The Planets*
Honegger, *Le Roi David*
Howard Hanson, Concerto for Organ, Strings, and Timpani
Poulenc, Concerto for Organ, Timpani, and Strings
Saint-Saëns, Symphony No. 3
Ernest Schelling, *A Victory Ball*
Richard Strauss, *Also sprach Zarathustra*
Joseph Wagner, *Variations on an Old Form*
Weinberger, Polka and Fugue from *Schwanda*

Chapter 34

SCORING FOR FULL ORCHESTRA

Scoring for full orchestra becomes a synthesis of the previous study-work carried out for each section. It calls for a review and reappraisal of instrumental values heretofore considered within sec-

Introduction
Scoring Chorals
The Composer's Approach
Short Scores

tional limitations. This expanded creative process deals with multiple instruments and voice parts with an enlarged scope of combinations and potentialities. Of necessity, it requires the acquisition of some totally new and different idiomatic playing styles quite apart from those associated with sectional arrangements and settings. Instruments acquire new standards of diversification when combined in orchestral settings. Playing techniques generally remain intact but scoring values change quite radically at times, in keeping with enlarged voice textures and timbre blendings. Likewise, scoring plans should remain sufficiently flexible to accommodate the demands made by the instrumentation for both large and small orchestras.

Practical orchestration, as outlined herein, seeks to provide the means for acquiring a scoring technique which can function with fundamental soundness without sacrificing artistic standards. The intrinsic value and artistic worth are not measured by its grade of difficulty. Nor is orchestral complexity synonymous with quality or profundity! The desideratum is orchestration which will sound with perfect clarity as a result of idiomatic settings arranged with good tonal balance. And, this technical process can be creative without being academically dull. It is not rule-bound, but creative work in all branches of art requires discipline if it is to reach its full potential. In short, orchestration is the clothing of musical ideas and textures with appropriate instrumental timbres and tonal weights which add definition and dimension.

Students of orchestration should avoid the pitfall of superficial thinking which establishes notes and music as being synonymous. Notes are nothing more than the *symbols* for sound! They are the still-life aspects of music. The orchestrator's task is to ceaselessly develop his perceptive faculties to a point where the visual symbols of notation become inseparably associated with gradation and variation of sound and timbre. This is an acquired skill indispensable to the successful orchestrator and conductor. The orchestrator must be able to read and hear a score with the objective eyes and ears of an impersonal conductor, for it is the conductor, and not the orchestrator, who must translate musical notation into living sound.

Previous study devoted to each section of the orchestra has included idiomatic settings of *America* as a representative four-part choral. These examples had few changes of voice texture and minimum doublings. Scoring chorals for full orchestra requires maximum tonal spreads and considerable doubling, as given in Examples I-27c and d. The same distinctions of timbre established for sectional scoring are continued for large and small instrumentations.

Example O-1a

America

Example O-1b

America

The approach to scoring varies with the individual composer. Some sketch their material for one piano (two or four hands) or two pianos. Others prefer to work from a short score or to score directly without any preliminary sketches. In this connection, it should be noted that those using the piano medium do so without necessarily resorting to pianistic idioms. Any of these working methods is justified if they bring about the desired results. The composer or orchestrator, working from a piano original, has a decidedly different problem, since the pianistic idioms must first be broken down in terms of orchestral textures and spacings. Although the *Reference Chart* was designed specifically for this latter type of orchestration, its application, as illustrated by the examples, can be equally helpful in arranging orchestral sketches for any instrumentation.

Much of the previous study has been directed toward stressing the importance of achieving idiomatic orchestral structure as the first indispensable prerequisite to scoring plans. All instrumental considerations should remain flexible until proper structural dispositions of melody, harmony, and rhythm have been satisfactorily decided upon. Coordinating and supplementing factors of secondary melodies, sustained elements, and various forms of ornamentation can then be examined with a clearer perspective. With experience, the creative process complements the more practical aspects of technique. A constructive habit is to proceed from the known to the unknown.

All preliminary work can be facilitated by writing out a condensed short score on three or four staves without transpositions. With it, the range, scope, and style of each component part can be separated sufficiently to permit a proper appraisal of the fluidity of each strand of the structural texture. It also is a distinct aid in promoting orchestral thinking along *horizontal* lines.

The following examples include these recommended tenets, and have been arranged to clarify their four principal elements: (1) melody, (2) rhythmic design, (3) middle harmonies, and (4) bass parts.

Example O-2

Example O-3

Example O-4

Example O-5a

Example O-5a *(continued)*

The short score is also helpful in developing the *visual* aspects of scoring as it affects the creative process. For example, the treble parts in the Moore piece have greater continuity by continuing the two-voice duet for the full excerpt. The method used for the extraction of these parts comes under the heading of Melodies with Large Melodic Skips and Dividing the Melodic Line in the *Reference Chart*. The sustained harmony and bass parts are more or less standard for music in the homophonic style. However, the short score reveals contrapuntal possibilities not superficially apparent in the original piano part. The addition of a third voice, as a canon in the tenor range, is one means of increasing part interest without detriment to the treble melodic lines. This change in melodic texture automatically forces a reappraisal of the harmonic structure. In this revised version (Example O-5b), sustained harmony and bass parts would smother the canon by their tonal thickness. Poor balance can be improved by rewriting the parts for *pizzicato* strings and/or harp. Contrasting timbres for the three melodies would be highly desirable.

Example O-5b

From this comparison of styles it can be assumed that sustained harmony parts occur quite regularly in homophonic music, while polyphonic textures require relative freedom from sustained parts if the play of the contrapuntal lines is to have clarity and fluidity. Polyphonic music needs the quality of transparency; homophonic music's effectiveness frequently depends upon the scoring of well-balanced harmonic progressions.

Chapter 35

THE REFERENCE CHART OF
KEYBOARD IDIOMS AND PATTERNS
APPLIED TO SCORING FOR
FULL ORCHESTRA

Full orchestra scoring of the major entries in the *Reference Chart* utilizes the same basic methods as the sectional models, but frequently with revised objectives. A reevaluation of idiomatic procedures is necessary as each instrument's technical capacities and tonal potentialities are more variable in mixed-timbre combinations. The multiple use of wind instruments is in itself a change from sectional scoring which cannot be ignored. Tonal strengths and weights become doubly significant in scoring solo wood-winds with full string sections. Balanced orchestral sonority is the product of well-placed and spaced melodic and harmonic elements which recognize instrumental limitations and fixed tonal ratios.

In all scoring plans the quality of *tonal balance* is of paramount importance. In this connection, the student orchestrator should review the concepts of the foreground and background analogy as given in Chap. 4. The relative tonal strengths and weights of the wind instruments are particularly sensitive in developing profile and definition for principal and secondary melodic lines. *Tutti* scoring, without the heavier brasses, can also be seriously unbalanced by faulty arrangement of the upper wood-winds. In brief, technical matters of range, style, and tonal intensity require revised objectives in scoring for full orchestra not normally encountered in sectional arrangements.

The following models, chosen from the *Reference Chart,* complete the cycle of evolution from strings, through the winds, to full orchestra. The instrumentation, in each instance, has been selected in accordance with the demands of the music: its composer, style texture, and characteristics.

Other models which were peculiarly applicable to sectional scoring have been omitted except as they occur as secondary considerations.

Although each example used serves to illustrate a specific major entry in the *Reference Chart,* it will be observed that other divisions of the *Chart* are constant factors in the complete scoring plans. These dual entries are of prime significance as they demonstrate, with tangible evidence, the scoring potentialities to be found in each piece. To realize the full musical implications in each orchestral sketch is to achieve craftsmanship of high merit.

Scoring conceptions for full orchestra may vary quite radically from those devised for sectional settings but, as always, the music itself should serve as a guide for the scope of its stylistic features. With experience, it will become apparent that certain formulas in technical matters remain fairly consistent and reliable. Once these technicalities have been mastered, the orchestrator is free to liberate his imaginative and creative processes in accordance with the musical values inherent in each piece.

I. BROKEN INTERVALS

I-1. Broken Octaves

(Sustained Intervals, VII-2; Melodic Settings, III-5)

Example O-6

Example O-6 *(continued)*

1. Broken octaves played as repeated notes in the strings will acquire additional coherence and sonority if doubled by *legato* wood-winds.

2. As dynamic intensity increases, ranges and sustained parts can increase proportionately. The heavier tonal weights (brasses), are normally reserved for the strongest points of gradual *crescendos*. This scoring plan, if applied in reverse order, is reliable for gradual *diminuendos*.

I-2. Broken Octaves with Embellishments
(Sustained Intervals, VII-2; Outlining, III-2)

Example O-7

Beethoven
Sonata, Op. 10, No. 3

Example 0-7 *(continued)*

1. This passage for full orchestra can have the embellished octaves played literally by the violins, with the flutes and clarinets outlining. The resulting dissonances will not be strident when scored for *contrasting* timbres.

2. The sustained horn and timpani parts add cohesiveness to the harmonic progressions.

3. The sustained bassoons and *pizzicato* bass parts for the first four measures are a good combination in the softer dynamic levels.

4. In the last four measures, the wood-winds are divided between outlining the embellished octaves and carrying on the principal melodic line. Notice the viola doubling this part as a change from constant harmonic figurations. In this connection, the orchestrator should seek diversification of melodic settings so that they do not become stereotyped.

1-4. Broken Sixths

(Interval Repetitions, V; Large Harmonic Gaps, VII-1)

Example O-8

Example O-8 *(continued)*

1. The non-*legato* eighth notes in the violins are absorbed by the wood-winds to create an over-all *legato* effect.

2. Sustained harmony parts are not desirable here as the texture is essentially three-part horizontal writing.

3. The three-octave bass part amply dispenses with the need for any middle-range harmonic fillers.

II-1. Left-hand Broken Chords in Close Position

(Sustained Intervals and Chords, VII-2; Melodic Settings, III-5; Antiphonal Effects, XI)

Example O-9

1. The clarinets are excellent for sustaining second-violin and viola parts in the middle register, especially when the dynamics are in the softer levels.

2. The added flute part embellishes the short *crescendo* without over-emphasis.

3. Occasional canonic imitation, as in the oboe part, increases part interest, particularly at phrase endings.

4. The sustained horn part serves as a harmonic binder in the middle register.

Example O-10

The oboe and horn in octaves combine well in sustaining common harmonic tones. Fifths of triads and seventh chords are best for this purpose.

Example O-11

Mozart
Sonata No. 3

Example O-11 *(continued)*

1. Increased instrumental sonority is in proportion to the increased dynamic tonal spread.

2. The scoring here makes use of the horn-trumpet-timpani combination for the conventional building up of the cadence.

3. Alternating choirs are employed for contrast in the last measures.

4. The horns in measures five and six retain parts usually identified with the natural type. For music of a later style, the parts would be in unison with the second clarinet and first bassoon.

5. The wood-winds at (1) and (2) illustrate a simple means of giving these parts slight voice independence without obscuring the real melodic line in the violins.

6. Trills in the string basses are cumbersome at best and are ordinarily omitted (3).

II-2. Left-hand Broken Chords in Open Position

(Outlining, III-2; Sustained Notes, VII-2; Melodic Settings, III-5)

Example O-12

1. The entrance of the wood-winds in the third measure creates timbre contrast for the entering third voice. It is a good scoring plan for passages of this kind.

2. The horn part has been developed from the descending chromatic top notes of the broken chords.

3. The viola and cello parts clarify and maintain the original piano figuration.

II-3. Broken Chords Spaced for Two Hands

(Sustained Chords, VII-2; Melodic Settings, III-5)

Example O-13

Example O-13 *(continued)*

1. The harmonic structure of the broken chords spaced for two hands has been reduced to part writing for the wood-winds. This reduction serves as a practical scoring device for sustaining harmonic progressions in this category.

2. The dialogue for the wood-winds in the last four measures provides contrast for the figuration originating in the strings.

3. Dissonances which resolve to consonances, as in the ninth measure, are quite frequent in orchestral part writing. Their definition is clearest when set in contrasting timbres. Dissonances in a single timbre have a strong "bite," especially in the double reeds.

II-4. Broken Chords in Right Hand with Implied Melodic Line

(Outlining, III-2; Dividing a Melodic Line, III-3;
Sustained Chords, VII-2; Antiphonal Effects, XI)

Example O-14

Example 0-14 (*continued*)

Example O-14 *(continued)*

1. The wind instruments in this setting have parts derived from a reduced version of the melodic and harmonic progressions of the triplet figure. These parts, played *legato,* provide clarity and solidity to the shifting ranges of the triplets.

2. The typical chord progressions for the natural horns with bassoons in the first four measures provide a good opportunity for an antiphonal effect with the higher wood-winds. Overlapping these two units reduces

the impression of blocked chords by the continuous flow of the progressions, notwithstanding the merging of different timbres for each new phrase. This principle of overlapping phrase entrances and endings can be of great value wherever and whenever long, smooth-flowing melodic lines, with different timbres, are desirable.

3. The repeated non-*legato* string chords in the first four measures are quite common with wind instruments, especially in the works of Classic composers.

4. The effect of antiphonal choirs, starting in the sixth measure, follows both the rhythmic pattern and *tessitura* changes present in the piano score.

5. The outlining of wood-winds in the last two measures is another illustration of dissonances resulting from part writing.

6. The interplay of the first violins with the seconds and violas continues the antiphonal idea within the string section. Here, too, alternating string parts can work to avoid monotony by creating interest with each new entrance of thematic material as it occurs.

II-5. Broken Chords with Blocked Melodic and Rhythmic Patterns

(Chord Repetitions, V; Sustained Chords, VII-2;
Large Harmonic Gaps, VII-1; Voice Leading, IX)

Example O-15

Beethoven
Sonata, Op. 10, No. 3

Example O-15 (continued)

Example O-15 *(continued)*

1. This passage with its *stretto* effect (overlapping thematic material in a steadily mounting *crescendo,* frequently over a pedal point), is easily reduced to *legato* part writing for the wood-winds. The strings are idiomatically set for the continuous non-*legato* eighth-note repetitions.

2. The retarded entrances of the horns and trumpets serve to build the sonority for the *stretto* through the prolonged sounding of the keynote D.

3. The total tonal spread expands proportionately to the increase of the dynamic level.

4. Orchestrations of music in the styles of the later Romantic and Modern composers would frequently have the bassoons and horns playing the thirds in the ninth and tenth measures. This addition, for the purpose of strengthening these parts, may be optional and conditioned by the full characteristics of each *tutti*.

III. Melodic Lines and Figurations
(Large Melodic Skips, III-1; Outlining a Melodic Line, III-2;
Large Harmonic Gaps, VII-1; Sustained Chords, VII-2)

Example O-16

1. In divided melodic lines set for mixed timbres, it is advisable to maintain consistently the divided parts in the same sections for com-

plete phrases. Here, the flutes and oboes, in relatively high *tessituras,* have sufficient tonal strength to offset the full string background.

2. The typical piano hand spread of the first measure, which converges toward harmonic close-position chords in the last measure, is approximated in the structural arrangement of the complete orchestral parts. The basic harmonic progressions are given to the bassoons and horns. These parts fill in the harmonic gaps of the first measure and continue sustaining the principal notes of the figure.

3. The clarinets sustain and define the descending violin parts. These thirds complete the full harmonic implications of the excerpt.

4. An element of contrast results from the separation of the melodic and harmonic divisions.

5. The contrabass *pizzicato* outlines the bass line and rhythmic pattern of the original left-hand part with the full harmonic implication of the figuration carried out by the combined bassoon and horn parts. It further clarifies the cross-rhythm effect (6/4 and 3/2) between the treble and bass parts of this excerpt. Outlining the cello part in this instance would distort and misrepresent the intentions of the composer.

III-3. Dividing a Melodic Line

(Contrast Problems, III-5; Antiphonal Effects, XI)

Example O-17

1. By dividing this melodic line into two parts, a uniform four-voice texture can be maintained throughout the complete phrase.

2. This scoring illustrates the principle of securing contrast by means of alternating the sections antiphonally. It may also be used to good advantage for mixed timbres within the wind sections.

III-4. Melodic Lines with Repeated Note Patterns

(Implied Bass Parts, IV; Single-note Repetitions, V;
Sustained Intervals, VII-2; Antiphonal Effects, XI)

Example O-18

Beethoven
Sonata, Op. 10, No. 3

Example O-18 *(continued)*

Example O-18 *(continued)*

1. The *stretto* character of this passage requires a gradual accumulation of instrumental strength to support the expanding range and dynamic level.

2. This excerpt becomes clearer for scoring purposes after its component parts have been isolated according to their respective functional designs. This can be accomplished by reducing each measure to horizontal part writing.

3. Each complete phrase, starting on the second beat of the first four measures, establishes the harmonic progression from which the repeated notes and the bass parts can be extracted.

4. Particular attention should be given to the scoring plan used for the addition of the wood-winds in building up the short canonic imitations and sustained, extended pedal points.

Example O-19

Granados
Danza Triste, Op. 5

Example O-19 *(continued)*

1. In this scoring, it is possible to sustain the string parts in the wood-winds to good advantage.

2. The added resonance in the harmony parts permits the octave melody without a loss of balance.

3. Note the continuation of the bassoon figure in the flute.

4. The rhythmic figure in the tambourine is derived from the melody.

V. SINGLE-NOTE, INTERVAL, AND CHORD REPETITIONS

(Contrasts, III-5; Sustained Notes and Intervals, VII-2)

Example O-20

1. The structural design of this passage has two dissimilar parts: continuous eighth-note figurations, and chords on the second half of each beat. With this division, it is possible to allot each part to a full section,

thereby maintaining uniform tonal strength for the complete passage. There may be times when the wood-winds could double outlined note repetitions of the strings (Example O-21), but in this instance they are needed to fill out the tonal spread of the chords. Contrast in tonal definition invariably results from this style of scoring.

Example O-21

Example O-21 *(continued)*

1. The trumpets, in the first measure, have the principal notes of the octaves to clarify the harmonic implications of the cadence.

2. The *fortissimo* dynamic in the first measure necessitates a maximum tonal spread while the sudden *forte-piano,* which follows, automatically suggests a contraction of these elements to a minimum degree.

3. A slightly expanded tonal range in the last two measures lends

contrast in keeping with the raised thirds in the bass register. The sustained *legato* parts in the treble, in unison with the *staccato* double reeds, create an additional tonal dimension without sacrificing the *staccato* effect of the original notation.

4. The sustained horn parts give tonal stability to the repeated notes in the *arco* strings.

VI. TWO- AND THREE-PART MUSIC

Homophonic

In considering scoring plans for the melody-harmony elements in homophonic music in two and three parts, weighing of relative strengths and weaknesses of each instrument and section is of prime importance. Combined violins, violas, and cellos are rarely given melodic lines in octaves if accompanied by the wood-winds unless the latter are reinforced by the brass, notably the horns. This condition does not hold if the accompaniment is mainly for the brass—with or without wood-winds. In addition, solo wood-winds or brasses can function well melodically when the harmonic texture is confined solely to the strings.

VI-1. Homophonic

(Broken Intervals, I-1; Contrast, III-5; Sustained Intervals, VII-2)

Example O-22

1. The structural arrangement previously developed for this excerpt in the string and wood-wind sections is quite adequate for the larger instrumentation given here.

2. Contrast for this phrase is possible through an exchange of timbres

as indicated. However, it should be noted that interchange of timbres, carried to excess, can cause distortion and loss of coherence.

3. The orchestrator planning alternations of timbres by full sections should evaluate each section's comparative tonal strengths and weights. The order of their succession is of real importance—the weak following the strong, or vice-versa. In this connection, it is of value to know that horns added to the wood-winds increase tonal weight without altering the character of the section. This same observation applies equally to added timpani parts.

Example O-23

1. Interplay of range and timbre for the melodic line contributes fresh interest to the confined range of the original melody *tessitura*.

2. The broken octaves in contrary motion for the flute, oboe, and bassoon add variety to the inverted pedal point.

3. The clarinets, combined with the sustained horn note, give additional resonance and balance in the middle register, thereby eliminating any impression of a heavy bass part.

VI-2. Polyphonic

Scoring polyphonic music for full orchestra follows the same general lines as those previously given under this category for the sections. Inclusion of the heavier brass and percussion instruments for music with formalized counterpoint (fugues and *fugatos*) is dependent upon its musical characteristics, style, texture, and dynamics. Indiscriminate doublings of the brass, merely to promote volume, are, under most conditions, highly inadvisable and undesirable. Such doublings are feasible only when the thematic material lends itself to idiomatic treatment. The percussion instruments for this category are likewise limited to infrequent rhythmic emphasis for music usually far removed from Classic conceptions and formalities. For a comparison of scoring styles in this classification, see Weiner's orchestration of the Fugue in Bach's Toccata and Fugue in C major and Weinberger's Fugue from his opera *Schwanda*.

Style Mixtures

Orchestrating style mixtures for full orchestra follows the same structural arrangements previously given for sectional scoring. The basic problem here is one of keeping the character of each style intact while securing balanced contrasts with multiple timbre blendings. To accomplish this, the tonal strength, weight, and intensity of each melodic line should be examined and balanced according to its separate and combined importance in each musical context. In addition, the points of contact, blending these two dissimilar styles, should avoid the impression of abrupt conflict except when indicated by the given dynamics. Music symphonically conceived has frequently an interplay of style mixtures. The orchestrator's task is to differentiate the scoring for the style mixtures and to seek a smooth blending in the process.

VI-3. Style Mixtures

(Melodic Settings: Contrasts, Comparative Strengths, Repeated Phrases, III-5; Sustained Intervals, VII-2)

Example O-24

Example O-24 *(continued)*

Example O-24 *(continued)*

Example O-24 *(continued)*

1. A sharp attack for isolated *sforzandos* and accents can be secured by a judicious use of unison doublings. It is a scoring device for notes of some duration, and appropriate for short phrases only.

2. The introduction of the homophonic style in measure nine permits sustained harmonic parts and a greater scope for doubling the melodic line.

3. An exchange of wood-wind timbres, starting with the clarinet entrance in the sixteenth measure, creates a diversified coloring for the melody which culminates in the final octaves of the last four measures. As arranged, these last six measures have greater interest than if played solely by the first violins.

VII. SPACING PROBLEMS IN THE MIDDLE REGISTER
(Contrasts, III-5; Large Harmonic Gaps, VII-1;
Sustained Notes, VII-2; Voice Leading, IX)

Example O-25

Edward MacDowell
In the Woods, Op. 28, No. 1

1. The structural plan here is basically the same as that given for Example S-44. The main difference is the added filler in the violins for the first two measures.

2. The oboe-clarinet duet, giving way to the clarinet solo in the third measure, has contrast value and places its less reedy timbre advantageously for the descending melody of the last measures.

3. The harp and bell parts add a touch of color without distorting the balance of the passage.

4. Notice the interpolated dynamics for the clarinet starting on A in the second measure. They have been inserted here so the solo phrase on the first beat of the third measure can start with a natural inflection upon taking over the lead from the oboe.

VIII. CONTRAST PROBLEMS CONDITIONED BY DYNAMICS

(Melodic Settings, III-5; Sustained Notes, VII-2;
Obbligatos, X; Dance Forms, XIII)

Example O-26

Chopin
Valse, Op. 34, No. 2

Example O-26 *(continued)*

1. These two settings illustrate one of the most common and effective ways of securing contrast for phrase repetitions at different dynamic levels. Contrast, with unchanging dynamics, may be secured with the juxtaposition of dissimilar timbres. In very loud passages, extended ranges—plus the freer use of doublings and fillers with the heavier tonal weights (brasses and percussion)—provide the chief means of increasing sonority and volume.

2. The scoring at [a] includes an *obbligato* developed similarly to that given in Example S-48c. Its position in the tenor range here permits greater clarity with the melody than if placed in different instruments above and/or crossing the treble parts as given.

3. **Note.** Grace notes occurring as part of a melody should be retained —without alteration—whenever practical. However, grace notes which are a pianistic device for completing chord spellings (see Example O-26), should not be included in orchestral parts. Rolled chords, as found in piano music, do not have practical counterparts in orchestration other than their rendition by the harp or the piano when the latter is used as an orchestral instrument.

IX. VOICE LEADING

The subject of voice leading, discussed in detail in Chaps. 10 and 11, continues as a vital consideration in working with larger instrumentations. It is particularly important for melodic phrases to be played in their entirety by one instrument whenever continuity of line is desired. In instances where melodies—or counterpoints—exceed normal ranges, overlapping and continuation by an instrument with the same timbre becomes a practical solution. As previously stated, chord positions, and their voice parts, should be viewed horizontally with consistent part writing.

X. OBBLIGATO OR ADDED SECONDARY PARTS ARRANGED FROM HARMONIC PROGRESSIONS

The orchestrator is free to use *obbligatos* when appropriate. In the tenor register they need fairly heavy tonal weight to be heard, especially in loud passages.

Figuration of simple melodies, the opposite of "Outlining a Melodic Line, III-2," can be quite effective in the high treble when arabesques can supply added vivacity and movement to passages otherwise rather colorless and dull. The student can experiment with this style of writing in many of the examples given in the *Workbook*.

XI ANTIPHONAL EFFECTS
Melodic Settings, III-5; Spacing Problems, VII-1)

Example O-27

1. The number of voice parts have been increased to consistently carry out the fullest chord representation indicated by the composer.

2. The string *pizzicato* will balance the wood-winds—without horns.

3. The octave skip in the last measure is pianistic rather than orchestral. It needs the chord for harmonic balance.

XII. TREMOLO TYPES

Previous study of tremolo types has shown the possible styles and notations for the strings and the wood-winds. Brass instruments were not considered for this effect other than for their idiomatic but restricted use of flutter tonguing.

Tremolo types scored for the full orchestra can be divided into two categories: those scored for either the strings or the wood-winds—without doublings—and those which have sustained doublings of the basic notations. Doublings, so used, are regularly given to the wood-winds and/or the brasses while the strings carry out the tremolos (see Examples I-14a and b). Strings are not used ordinarily to sustain or support wood-wind tremolos, although string tremolos, wood-wind trills, and brass flutter tonguing may be combined occasionally when extraordinary coloristic effects are sought.

Sustaining the basic notation of string tremolos can be an effective means of clarifying harmonic elements (single notes, intervals, or chords); of securing tonal depth, dimension, or solidity; and of increasing volume in a variety of tonal colors and dynamic levels.

XIII. DANCE FORMS

(Broken Chords, II-2; Outlining, III-2; Melodic Settings, III-5; Style Mixtures, VI-3; Spacing Problems, VII-1; Contrast Problems Conditioned by Dynamics, VIII; Voice Leading, IX)

Example O-28

Prokofiev
Gavotte, Op. 12, No. 2

Example O-28 (*continued*)

Example O-28 *(continued)*

1. *Legato* wood-wind and detached string parts—in unison—occur rather frequently. This style of doubling gives depth and substance to these parts obtainable in no other way.

2. The mixed homophonic and polyphonic styles of this excerpt necessitated clear definition of the harmonic and contrapuntal parts through the use of balanced tonal strengths and adjusted dynamics. Harmonic progressions in this kind of music should be scored so that they will be complete in themselves, without assistance from the counterpoints.

3. The bells at the beginning outline the melody.

4. The interpolated *legato* phrasing, starting in measure eight, aids in contrasting the detached figuration in the strings.

5. Note the carrying out of the complete descending tenor part (horns) with its characteristic grace notes.

6. Further observe the method used to expand and contract tonal spreads and weights in keeping with changing dynamics.

7. The disposition of the melody-harmony parts in the treble, starting in measure five, should be studied in detail.

8. Notice the exchange of the melody in the trumpet parts in the last full measure.

Chapter 36

CONCLUSION

Differences in Source Material
Choral Orchestration
Conducting Technique for the
Orchestrator
Rehearsal Numbers
Cuing
Selected List of Orchestral
Transcriptions

The previous subject matter has presented many of the most frequently encountered scoring problems along with a variety of possible solutions. The purpose has been to provide working backgrounds which could be conducive to purposeful, explorative, and creative orchestral thinking.

The composer, scoring from orchestral sketches, has somewhat different methods of procedure than the orchestrator working from original music for piano or organ as source material. In the latter case, suitable provisions must be made to accommodate the vast differences in tone production between the two instruments. A single note in the middle register of the piano, if played on the organ, may be expanded as much as four octaves by the use of couplers and stop extensions. There is also the non-sustaining percussive tone of the piano and the sustaining but non-percussive tone of the organ to be reckoned with. These are two elements of major difference having a direct bearing on the structural distribution of the voice parts. Dynamics, therefore, are somewhat misleading and decidedly comparative in working with music for these two instruments.

Likewise, the orchestrator should be keenly aware of structural variations and timbre subtleties encountered when scoring for small and large instrumentations. Orchestral resonance is constantly subject to changing structural spacings and instrumental distributions in accordance with the playing potentialities of each section. Nowhere is the importance of these two elements more apparent than in the scoring of *tuttis* for instrumentations of varying sizes. Not only do instrumental values become involved, but their alternations and doublings remain constant factors to be dealt with according to the musical scope of each piece.

The *Reference Chart of Keyboard Idioms and Patterns* is uniquely adaptable to the scoring of accompaniments of choral works originally for piano or organ. In working with these media, it is desirable to first determine the purpose and scope of the orchestral accompaniment and the probable size and skill of the chorus. Once these details have been approximately decided, they can prove helpful to the orchestrator in determining such matters as style, scope, instrumentation, and grade of difficulty.

For all practical purposes, choral accompaniments can be divided into two types: those with independent melodic lines and textures, and those which double one or more vocal parts in conjunction with supporting harmonizations. The orchestrator's task in transcribing both types is to determine to what extent vocal parts will be doubled, either in unison or in octaves, and to select instruments which most naturally can support each vocal line. Doubling of choral parts by orchestral instruments occurs most frequently under the following conditions:

1. Significant extended passages with difficult vocal intervals requiring extra instrumental support
2. Parts which should be decidedly prominent
3. Melodic progressions in weak vocal *tessituras*
4. Involved *fugatos* of significant length
5. Peak climaxes with tonal power and brilliance

The choice of the doubling instruments will be dependent upon dynamics, ranges, and the musical character of each phrase. Instruments doubling voice parts have maximum rhythmic reductions. Notes are not repeated, as in the vocal parts, because of the prosody.

Occasionally, harmonic progressions permit the insertion of notes as cues anticipating unusually tricky choral entrances. These advanced notes serve as a steadying device to insure pitch recognition for amateur choral groups and are particularly desirable preceding entrances with intricate harmonic progressions for very large choruses. The majority of these points for choral orchestration are well illustrated by a comparison of the vocal-piano editions and full scores of Beethoven's *Missa Solemnis* and the Verdi *Requiem*.

Experienced teachers believe that students of composition and orchestration should have required courses in the practical aspects of conducting. There can be no doubt that familiarity with the technique of the baton, score reading, and orchestral balance, as major objectives, assumes broader meaning and significance when assimilated and integrated with a flexible scoring technique. There is also the advantage of gaining a conductor's objectivity in appraising scoring details, which is a valuable asset. The acquisition of this kind of background experience helps to prepare the orchestrator for a detached and impersonal evaluation of his work. It also gives a direct insight into the technical phases of a conductor's art in transforming lifeless notation into living sound. In practice, it further exposes and discloses the shortcomings, weaknesses, and strengths of a score which might otherwise appear to be both adequate and faultless. Preparation gained in this way enables the composer-orchestrator to appear before an orchestra with added confidence and practical knowledge. The bibliography lists three source books on conducting that are of interest and value for supplementary self-education on this subject.

Two utilitarian details of orchestration remain to be considered. The first is the addition of rehearsal numbers or letters in the finished score and parts. They are usually placed at intervals of ten to fifteen measures apart at the beginning of *tuttis,* difficult passages, and after many measures of thin scoring. In short, rehearsal numbers should be placed and spaced to simplify repetitions during rehearsals.

The second item concerns the optional addition of cued parts to substitute for possible missing instruments. Commercial orchestrations designed for school and amateur groups resort to a system of cuing and cross-cuing which places essential passages in more than one part and section. An important oboe solo may, with this system, be found as a cue in the flute, clarinet, or muted trumpet parts. Oboes, bassoons, and third and fourth horns are the most likely instruments to be unavailable in school and amateur orchestras. These parts are usually cued as follows: oboes in muted trumpets, clarinets, or flutes; bassoons in muted trombones or saxophones; and the horns in trumpets and/or trombones or saxophones.

The orchestrator will find it helpful to have cued parts in the score written in an ink of contrasting color to the regular notation. Cued parts have all note stems pointing upward regardless of their positions on the staff. In cross-cuing, simultaneous notation for actual parts have all stems facing downward. Should this part be silent, full-measure rests are placed below the staff. The orchestrator should fully recognize and understand that cued parts are functional concessions and that their use automatically destroys subtleties of tonal color and balance. They are at best makeshift substitutions of dubious distinction.

Finally, the orchestrator's attention is directed toward the following selected listing of published orchestral transcriptions of music originally composed for keyboard instruments. There is much practical knowledge to be gained from a study of the note-to-note process of transcription where all the details of changing textures, spacings, doublings, and fillers can be minutely examined and compared. This study will be of use in the application of all the entries of the *Reference Chart*. It similarly could form a tangible source of reference material of proven worth and value, since the majority of the titles are available on records.

SELECTED LIST OF PUBLISHED ORCHESTRAL TRANSCRIPTIONS OF MUSIC FOR KEYBOARD INSTRUMENTS

Composer	Orchestrator	Medium	Title
Albéniz	Arbós	Piano	*Iberia*
Bach	Ormandy	Organ	*Sleepers Awake*
Bach	Respighi	Organ	Passacaglia and Fugue in C minor
Bach	Stokowski	Organ	Toccata and Fugue in D minor
Bach	Weiner	Organ	Toccata and Fugue in C major
Balakirev	Casella	Piano	*Islamey*
Barber	Barber	Piano	*Souvenirs*
Bartók	Bartók	Piano	*Hungarian Peasant Songs*
Bartók	Bartók	Piano	*Roumanian Folk Dances*
Beethoven	Weingartner	Piano	Sonata, Op. 106
Brahms	Brahms	Two pianos	*Variations on a Theme by Haydn*
Brahms	Parlow	Piano duet	*Hungarian Dances,* Nos. 5 and 6
Brahms	Rubbra	Piano	*Variations and Fugue on a Theme by Handel*
Casella	Casella	Piano duet	*Pupazzetti*
Chabrier	Mottl	Piano	*Bourrée fantasque*
Chopin	Glazunov	Piano	*Chopiniana*
Debussy	Ansermet	Piano duet	*Epigraphes antiques*
Debussy	Busser	Piano duet	*Petite Suite*
Debussy	Caplet	Piano	*Children's Corner*
Debussy	Caplet	Piano	*La Boite à joujoux*
Debussy	Molinari	Piano	*L'Isle joyeuse*
Debussy	Ravel	Piano	*Danse*
Dvořák	Dvořák	Piano duet	*Slavonic Dances*
Fauré	Rabaud	Piano duet	*Dolly* Suite
Franck	Pierné	Piano	Prélude, Choral, and Fugue
Frescobaldi	Giannini	Organ	*Frescobaldiana*
Grieg	Grieg	Piano	*From Holberg's Time* (strings) *Norwegian Dances*
Grieg	Grieg	Piano	*Lyric Suite*
Griffes	Griffes	Piano	*The White Peacock*
Liszt	Liszt	Piano	*Mephisto Waltz*
Liszt	Muller-Berghaus	Piano	*Hungarian Rhapsody* No. 2
Liszt	Muller-Berghaus	Piano	Polonaise in E
MacDowell	Altschuler	Piano	*Sonata Tragica*
Milhaud	Milhaud	Piano	*Tango des Fratellini*
*Moussorgsky	Ravel	Piano	*Pictures at an Exhibition*

* The orchestral score contains the original piano version.

Composer	Orchestrator	Medium	Title
Ravel	Ravel	Piano	*Alborada del Gracioso*
Ravel	Ravel	Piano	*Le Tombeau de Couperin*
Ravel	Ravel	Piano duet	*Ma Mère l'oye*
Ravel	Ravel	Piano	*Minuet antique*
Ravel	Ravel	Piano	*Pavane*
Ravel	Ravel	Piano	*Valses nobles et sentimentales*
Satie	Debussy	Piano	*Gymnopédies*
Scarlatti, D.	Casella	Piano	Toccata, Bourrée, et Gigue
Schumann, R.	Konstaninoff	Piano	*Carnaval*
Shostakovitch	Stokowski	Piano	Prélude in E flat
Slonimsky	Slonimsky	Piano	*My Toy Balloon*
Stravinsky	Stravinsky	Piano duet	Suites Nos. 1 and 2
Turina	Turina	Piano	*Danzas Fantasticas*
Weber	Berlioz	Piano	*Invitation to the Dance*
Weber	Szell	Piano	*Perpetual Motion*

BIBLIOGRAPHY

ORCHESTRATION

Anderson, Arthur Olaf: *Practical Orchestration,* C. C. Birchard Co., Boston, 1929.

Berlioz, Hector, and Richard Strauss: *Treatise on Instrumentation,* E. F. Kalmus, Inc., New York, 1948.

Forsyth, Cecil: *Orchestration,* 2nd ed., The Macmillan Company, New York, 1935.

Heacox, Arthur E.: *Project Lessons in Orchestration,* Oliver Ditson Co., Boston, 1928.

Jacob, Gordon: *Orchestral Technique,* Oxford University Press, New York, 1931.

Kennan, Kent Wheeler: *The Technique of Orchestration,* Prentice-Hall, Inc., Englewood Cliffs, N.J., 1952.

Piston, Walter: *Orchestration,* W. W. Norton & Co., Inc., New York, 1955.

Read, Gardner: *Thesaurus of Orchestral Devices,* Pitman Publishing Corporation, New York, 1953.

Rimsky-Korsakov, Nicolas: *Principles of Orchestration,* 3rd ed., E. F. Kalmus, Inc., New York, 1938.

CONDUCTING

Bernstein, Martin: *Score Reading,* M. Witmark & Sons, New York, 1932.

Scherchen, Hermann: *Handbook on Conducting,* tr. M. D. Calvocoressi, Oxford University Press, New York, 1933.

Weingartner, Felix: *On the Performance of Beethoven's Symphonies,* E. F. Kalmus, Inc., New York, 2nd ed., 1916.

PUBLICATION CREDITS
FOR EXCERPTS OF PIANO MUSIC

The settings of the following compositions are used here by permission of the publisher, Oliver Ditson Company.

Capriccio, Op. 76, No. 8	Johannes Brahms
Sonata, Op. 5	
Rhapsody, Op. 79, No. 1	
Serious Variations, Op. 54	Felix Mendelssohn

The settings of the following compositions are quoted here by courtesy of the publisher, Edward B. Marks Music Corporation, New York City.

Danza Triste, Op. 5, No. 7	Enrique Granados
Gavotte, Op. 12, No. 2	Serge Prokofiev
Impromptu, Op. 142, No. 4	Franz Schubert
Moment Musical, Op. 94	
Polichinelle, Op. 3, No. 4	Serge Rachmaninov
Valse, Op. 10, No. 2	
Sous le palmier, Op. 232, No. 3	Isaac Albéniz

The settings of the following compositions:

Danse des Dryades	Valdimir Rebikov
Gavotte in B flat	Georg Friedrich Handel
Piece in A Major	Wilhelm Friedrich Bach
Sarabande	Arcangelo Corelli

are from the Fourth Solo Book by Angela Diller and Elizabeth Quaile, copyright 1924 by G. Schirmer, Inc. and are quoted here by permission of the copyright owner and publishers, G. Schirmer, New York.

Quotations and settings of other music in this category have been used through the courtesy of the publisher, Edward F. Kalmus, New York City.

INDEX